This Old House

➤ **SALVAGE-STYLE PROJECTS**

Amy R. Hughes

PHOTOGRAPHS BY KRISTINE LARSEN

I'm a junker.

And I suspect you are too. We're the ones scanning for hidden gems on trash day. Or directing our significant others to the nearest coffee shop while we rifle through hardware bins at the salvage yard. We're those drivers in the slow lane with paneled wood doors roped to the roof like 21st-century Clampetts.

It's not just the thrill of the hunt that compels us. We're taking that old stuff home and recycling it— the hardware used to hinge a new folding screen, and the door turned on its side and hung on the wall as a headboard. It's also the creativity that goes into crafting cool furniture for our homes that spurs us on, and the pride that comes from decorating with things we built ourselves. We're not just junkers, after all. We are makers and DIYers.

And our ranks are growing. Just witness the explosion of books, blogs, and TV shows touting the virtue of thrift and the value of making stuff with your hands. The urge to salvage and create is embedded in our DNA: As Americans, the tradition stretches to colonial times, when primitive furniture was often built from barn wood, packing crates, even old boat hulls.

I inherited the salvage gene from my mother, who was always turning things that had outlived their original function into something useful and kid, I played horse-drawn sleigh that she repurposed as a boot bench, and flipped through the records stored in the huge wood icebox that also housed the hi-fi. Today I do the same in my home, using an old commercial baker's rack to store serving dishes, and an apothecary cabinet as a bathroom étagère.

I've also made salvaging part of my job as an editor at *This Old House* magazine, where we champion the DIY approach. For the past 10 years, I've been making one-of-a-kind pieces out of reclaimed house parts and telling the stories of those historical details in a monthly column. This book is a continuation of that work and, I hope, an inspiration for you to start creatively repurposing stuff for your place, whether you're renting a studio apartment or fixing up a house of your own.

Inside you'll find 22 step-by-step projects for turning salvaged finds, such as porcelain faucet handles and wrought-iron window guards, into high-style, low-cost enhancements. All that's required of you are a sense of adventure, an eye for bargains, and a good set of tools. The last two I'll even help with, in the form of treasure-hunting tips and a guide to setting up your workshop.

Follow along, and you'll soon be transforming your home into an eclectic living space that not only reflects your love of old stuff reborn but showcases your handiwork too.

Amy

SALVAGE-STYLE PROJECTS

Getting Started

Creative Reuse Projects

60

8

72

16

120

92

TOH Reader Projects

Ideas for Interiors

WHERE TO FIND IT

7

What Is Salvage?

Salvage is just about anything that's been plucked from the ruins for reuse. But for the purposes of this book, it refers to rescued house parts, particularly those from the 1860s to the 1940s. That's when everything from kitchen sinks to stair spindles had a lot of character and was built to last out of quality materials such as Vermont slate and American chestnut.

The process of salvaging goes back thousands of years. The ancient Romans famously used marble columns from one tumbledown temple to erect another. In this country, you can find statuary that once decorated grand old train stations and post offices now marking the entrances to bridges and public libraries.

Salvagers like me work on a smaller scale, creatively repurposing old hardware, ironwork, and doors from demolished or remodeled houses into new furniture, storage pieces, and accessories for our own living spaces. It's a way to add vintage character to even the newest homes—and to keep alive the craftsmanship of those old Victorian-era Queen Annes and English-style Tudors long after they've vanished from the landscape.

Shopping for Salvage

➤➤ YOU CAN FIND OLD HOUSE PARTS AT SALVAGE YARDS, REUSE CENTERS, AND ANTIQUES FAIRS AND FLEA MARKETS. EACH SOURCE HAS ITS OWN UNIQUE FLAVOR, SELECTION, AND PRICING

Salvage Yards ➠

These vast indoor and outdoor emporiums are full of claw-foot tubs, stained-glass windows, exterior wood doors, marble mantels, iron fencing, period light fixtures, and lots and lots of hardware. Most dealers salvage the architectural details themselves, bidding for the rights to surgically remove them from houses and buildings slated for demolition. Some also purchase directly from homeowners and contractors undertaking a remodel. Of the various places to find old house parts, salvage yards are typically the priciest. You pay for the wide selection, and the option of turnkey service, which can include repair, refinishing, delivery, and sometimes even help with the installation in your home.

Salvage yards offer the widest selection of old house parts, from chandeliers and wall-hung sinks to wood doors and floorboards.

Where to find them

Just about every state has at least one salvage yard. But if you're unsure where the closest one is, ask a contractor; many buy reclaimed materials for restoration jobs. I've also compiled a resource guide in the back of this book. For a more complete listing of salvage yards, as well as antique-lumber and garden-ornament dealers, check the website of *Architectural Salvage News*, which puts out an annual directory that you can download.

Treasure hunting tips for salvage yards

- **Bring props.** Blueprints, room photos, pages torn from magazines, as well as items that need to be replaced or matched, are great to have on hand while *CONTINUED ON NEXT PAGE* you shop. That way it's easy to convey your vision to the salvage dealer and get help finding the right materials.

• **Ask for advice.** I've gotten some of my best creative-reuse ideas from salvage dealers. They've seen and done it all, and are great problem solvers. Some can even turn that old door into a coffee table for you—for a price.

• **Keep an open mind.** The fun of making new stuff out of salvage is that everything is ripe for reinvention. Carved-wood door casing can become a mirror frame, a medicine cabinet can double as a message center, and a kitchen sink can be transformed into an outdoor bar.

• **Shop with a pro.** If you don't plan on doing the work yourself, make sure that your contractor, architect, carpenter, or plumber is up to the task of working with and retrofitting the salvaged materials before you buy. Old house parts typically aren't returnable.

• **Know your measurements** for the room, space, or opening you need to fill. Unlike many new parts, which come in standard sizes, old ones were often custom built on-site or factory-made and sold via catalogs that predate modern construction codes.

• **Be prepared to get dirty.** I ruined my favorite white pants while sorting through crates of dust- and mortar-covered ceramic bathroom accessories. Granted, I like my toothbrush holder better than the pants, but it was a lesson: Always wear dark jeans and tees to the salvage yard. ***CONTINUED ON NEXT PAGE***

Negotiate on price but be fair.

HOW TO BARGAIN

Seldom should you pay sticker price. Whether you're at a salvage yard or a flea market, dealers expect you to ask for a discount, so don't be shy. Just be reasonable. Ten percent off is considered fair. For anything more, you'll need leverage. Buying in bulk—such as five stair spindles instead of one—or shopping in tandem with a friend can easily get you a package rate. Reputable dealers also welcome you to inspect for scratches, dents, or excessive wear. If you make a case that an item requires refinishing or a lot of work to retrofit, dealers will often negotiate further on price. I once got 30 percent off a 1930s pendant light because I explained that, in addition to rewiring it, I'd have to replace hard-to-find mounting hardware. It all starts with a respectful conversation.

MY FIELD BAG

➡ WHETHER YOU'RE SCOURING A SALVAGE YARD OR BRAVING CROWDS AND WEATHER AT AN OPEN-AIR FLEA MARKET, BRING ALONG THESE ESSENTIALS

1. Rain boots
Fairgrounds and salvage yards can be mud pits.

2. Water bottle
Keeps you hydrated while rummaging for vintage finds.

3. Sunglasses Cut glare when shopping during peak sun hours.

4. Hammer To tap in popped nails and tighten loose joints before transport.

5. Tape measure
For checking fit before you buy.

6. Hat Shades your face from the sun.

7. Raincoat
A packable jacket will keep you dry without weighing you down.

8. Wipes For washing up, and revealing maker's marks.

9. Sunscreen Wander around a flea market without SPF, and you will get burned.

10. Multitool
For screwing, pulling, prying, and sawing stuff.

11. Smartphone To take and e-mail photos, arrange deliveries, and compare prices online.

12. Hand sanitizer
There's no telling where this stuff's been.

13. Pad and pencil
For jotting down item numbers and measurements.

14. Mini pry bar
To pull rusty nails so you don't get stuck.

15. Flashlight
Brightens dark corners and puts details into focus.

16. Magnet Tells you the difference between brass (it won't stick) and plated metal.

17. Work gloves
To protect hands from sharp metal edges and splintered wood.

Antiques fairs offer great deals on salvage, such as this fireplace summer front.

Antiques Fairs and Flea Markets ➺

These events put everything on display, from ornately carved corbels and stained-glass windows to wingback chairs and highboy dressers, often at 50 percent off what you would pay at salvage yards and antiques stores. Dealers tend to price wares for quick sale because whatever doesn't get bought has to be packed up and carted away at their expense when the event's over. It's also about volume; wholesale prices allow them to sell large quantities to other dealers who are looking to replenish their store shelves.

How to find them The first place I look is the "What's happening" section of the local newspaper or weekly entertainment guide. Fair and flea-market listings are also posted online and in antiques and collectibles trade publications. Big promoters, such as Renningers and Stella Show Management, post schedules on their websites for the various events that they organize around the country. Fairs and fleas in warm climates happen year-round; the typical season is early spring to late summer.

Treasure hunting tips for antiques fairs and flea markets

• **Get there early.** The serious shoppers and antiques-store owners are the first ones through the gates, so consider your competition. If you are looking for something specific, such as a carved-wood mantel shelf, there may be just one.

• **Act fast.** You really can't say "I'll think about it" and come back later. I've learned the hard way, returning an hour later to find that the cast-brass door hardware I coveted had been snatched up.

• **Beware of fly-by-nights.** The best insurance against paying too much is to buy from established dealers. Ask how long she's been exhibiting at the fair. The good ones are always welcomed back by the organizers and return year after year.

• **Stay focused.** Make a list of the items you want, and keep your eyes peeled for just those items. It's easy to cast too wide a net and become overwhelmed when faced with hundreds of booths to look through.

• **Dress comfortably.** I wear good walking shoes and prepare for both blazing sun and sudden downpours.

• **Plan how you'll get it home.** Some fairs and fleas have a pack-and-ship booth, but most don't. If you buy something, it's up to you to haul it away. So don't forget where you parked the car! For large stuff like a pair of French doors, it's usually okay to pay in advance and ask the dealer to store the items for a few hours. Just get a receipt with the booth number and dealer's name so that you can go back and find it.

Reuse Centers ➤→

These warehouses are filled with gently used—and some new—building materials, such as kitchen cabinets and bifold doors, that might otherwise go in a landfill. These items, which are sold at low prices, end up at centers in different ways: Homeowners donate castoffs from renovation projects, contractors bring in surplus materials from job sites, and sometimes people donate entire houses so that they can be delicately "deconstructed" in order to salvage and resell all their parts.

How to find them Most centers are nonprofits with proceeds going to social or environmental causes. The best known are the ReStore outlets run by Habitat for Humanity, which posts a national directory on its website.

Treasure hunting tips for reuse centers

• **Dig deep.** Reuse centers specialize in newish house parts, but they do have old stuff, too. I once found an early 1900s five-panel solid-oak door buried in a stack of hollow-cores.

Items for sale at reuse centers range from roof tiles to windows.

• **Go often.** The stock at reuse centers is priced to move, so there's new stuff coming in daily.

• **Make a friend.** If there's something specific you're after, ask an employee to let you know if one comes in. I got a used 24-inch pro-style gas range for my remodeled kitchen by putting in a request for apartment-size appliances.

HOW TO SPOT A FAKE

➤➤ MY HARD-LEARNED TIPS FOR TELLING THE GENUINE ARTICLE FROM AN IMPOSTER

1.

Form an impression. Stand back and take a good look at the design, proportion, and materials. Then ask yourself if all the parts work together to create a harmonious whole. For instance, if a mantel's legs look too slender to support its wide shelf, it's likely a Frankenstein.

2.

Check the patina. It's a timeworn look developed from years of use—not by applying an antiquing solution or layering coats of new paint—that makes salvaged details so desireable. A true patina has a warm and variable surface; a faux finish can look too perfect.

3.

Look for a maker's mark. Some wood built-ins bear a carpenter's signature. But marks are more common on the backs of Victorian-era ceramic wall tiles and on the bases or hollow recesses of ornamental cast-iron planters, birdbaths, and fountains.

4.

Pick it up. The real deal is often heavy. Old fencing was made of hefty iron, not the light aluminum used today. Garden benches were carved from stone rather than molded from resins. For wood, it's the opposite: Solid stock weighs less than modern plywood.

5.

Consider the price. A high one is no guarantee of authenticity, but a super-low price usually is too good to be true. When in doubt, use your smartphone to do a little on-the-spot comparative analysis by checking what similar pieces sell for via online auction sites.

Setting Up Your Workshop

TO CRAFT NEW TREASURES OUT OF OLD MATERIALS, YOU'LL NEED A GOOD SET OF TOOLS. HERE'S WHAT I'VE GOT IN MY SHOP, AND WHAT YOU'LL SEE USED ON THE FOLLOWING PAGES

COMPOUND MITER SAW

RANDOM-ORBIT SANDER

CUT, SAND, SHAPE

Utility knife Its retractable blade scores and shaves wood, cuts cardboard boxes, and sharpens pencils in a pinch.

Power saws A circular saw's rotating toothed disk makes quick, straight cuts in wood. For angled cuts on wide moldings, use a compound miter saw. A jigsaw is the go-to saw for intricate curves and circles.

Straight-cut snips Heavy-duty scissors for cutting sheet metal.

Random-orbit sander A power sander that rotates and oscillates, allowing you to smooth wood surfaces without having to follow the grain pattern.

Chisel A must for cutting mortises, a chisel's beveled blade can dig out wood as well as shave and smooth the surface.

Block plane Rounds over sharp wood edges; trims and fits joints.

HAMMER AND NAILSET

DRIVE, PRY, SCRAPE

Hammer and nailset A 16-ounce curved-claw hammer is a versatile nail driver and puller. Use the nailset to recess fastener heads.

Rubber mallet More forgiving than a hammer's metal head, a rubber one lets you "persuade" pieces into place and shape metal around a substrate without marring surfaces.

Multi-bit screwdriver Interchangeable slotted and Phillips tips are typically stored in the driver's handle.

Drill/driver and bit kit This power tool can bore holes or drive screws, depending on the bit you use. A basic bit kit contains an assortment of different-size tips.

Prybar The light-duty Japanese-style ones remove delicate trim and pull nails.

Painter's tool Use it to scrape debris, spread putty, open paint cans—even crack a beer when the work's all done.

PAINTER'S TOOL

2-FOOT
LEVEL

MEASURE, LAYOUT

Tape measure A flexible steel ruler that's rigid when extended yet retracts into a compact coil you can clip to your tool bag or belt.
Levels To tell if a surface is level or plumb. Use a 2-foot level for hanging a large item, like a cabinet. A torpedo level is easier to handle for small stuff.
Squares Use an adjustable combination square to measure, mark cutlines, and check 90-degree corners. A framing square's large, fixed, L-shaped design is ideal for doing the same when working with bigger boards. A Speed Square can double as a guide for your circular saw.

MULTI-BIT
SCREWDRIVER

TIGHTEN, GRIP, PAINT

Pliers The adjustable jaws on tongue-and-groove pliers grip bolts and pipe fittings of various diameters. Needle-nose pliers reach into tight spaces. Linesman pliers grip small items, and cut wire.
Adjustable wrench For assembling anything with nuts and bolts. One with long handles offers extra leverage; short handles are best in tight spaces.
Clamps Bar clamps hold together wide pieces, such as the sides of a box. Spring clamps work like an extra set of hands to grip small pieces.
Paintbrushes For latex paint, use one with nylon or polyester bristles. For oil paint, a natural-bristle brush is best.
Caulk gun Squeezes out a neat bead of caulk or construction adhesive.

TONGUE-
AND-
GROOVE
PLIERS

KEEP
IT SAFE

Slipping on safety glasses and popping in earplugs are no-brainers for guarding against flying shards and loud noises in a workshop. But protecting yourself from lead—a serious yet less obvious danger— is tricky. The heavy metal, which was used in many coatings made before 1978, when it was banned as an additive, can be released as toxic dust when handling vintage house parts, particularly those caked in old paint. Here's how to guard against lead:

> **Work outdoors,** or seal off an indoor area with plastic sheeting to keep lead dust contained.
> **Wear a NIOSH-certified dust mask,** and put on an outer layer of clothing that you can toss in a bag so that dust is not tracked through the house.
> **Contain or strip the finish.** Lead paint is harmless if you encase it under new paint or a clear coat. To remove the old finish, use a gel stripper, which turns the paint into a paste-like film you can scrape off, then dispose of in a plastic trash bag. Never dry-scrape or sand; this releases lead dust into the air.
> **Clean thoroughly.** If working indoors, go over all surfaces with a vacuum equipped with a HEPA filter, which keeps fine lead dust particles out of the exhaust and the air. Then wet-mop with an all-purpose cleaner-degreaser to attract and stabilize any remaining lead dust.

USE
FAUCET HANDLES
TO MAKE A

Towel Rack

Creamy white faucet handles can double as stylish towel or robe hooks. All you've got to do is mount the old porcelain beauties on a board—I used salvaged barn siding, but any scrap wood will do—and hang the assembly on a bathroom wall. • For my project, I went a step further, adding a shelf supported by ornate cast-iron brackets, about $15 each at online housewares shops. This way I can stack fresh bath towels on top and hang wet ones to dry from the handles below. • I scored three cross-style handles at a salvage yard for $45, including the matching porcelain escutcheons that used to sleeve over the faucets' valve stems. The escutcheons came in handy again, but this time to hide the dummy door spindles on which each handle is mounted. You can find the spindles, which are typically used for interior French doors or closet doors that have fixed pull-type knobs, at home centers or locksmith shops for about $4 each. • Since there's no scalding water to worry about with this towel rack project, feel free to arrange your handles on the board any way you wish. But if you're a stickler for historical accuracy, the HOT one was always on the left.

Supplies

3 PORCELAIN HANDLES AND ESCUTCHEONS
BARN WOOD OR SCRAP BOARDS
2 SHELF BRACKETS
3 DUMMY SPINDLES
PENCIL
EPOXY
1 5/8-INCH TRIM-HEAD SCREWS

Tools

TAPE MEASURE
DRILL/DRIVER
1/16-INCH DRILL BIT
SCREWDRIVER
COMBINATION SQUARE

 1 HOUR $100   SKILL LEVEL: <u>EASY</u>

Start Here

Mark where
the shelf will go.
Trace a line on
the board where
its top shelf will sit
to figure out how
high to position the
supporting brackets
on either end.

Measure the mounting board.
Cut wood to size and use a tape measure to determine
the rough distance between each handle. I planned to
space mine evenly across the face of the board. Factor in
an extra inch on either side of the board for the brackets.

3 **4** **5**

**Determine
the bracket
locations.**
Position the
brackets 1 inch
in from the ends
of the mounting
board, with their
tops just below the
pencil line. Mark
where the brackets'
fasteners will go.

**Secure the
brackets.**
First, use your
drill/driver to
create pilot holes
for the fasteners.
Then use the
screws provided
with the brackets
to fasten the
supports to the
board.

Mark layout lines to determine handle placement.
Use your pencil to lightly draw a horizontal line across the
center of the mounting board. Then mark evenly spaced
vertical lines through the horizontal one. The handles will go
where the lines intersect.

⟫→
Steps 6-9

Tool School

I've got a good eye, but not that good. To ensure
straight layout lines, I use a COMBINATION SQUARE,
a staple in woodworkers' tool kits. Place the edge of
the square head (the part with the handle) against
the board's edge, and guide a pencil along the
ruler's perpendicular blade, as shown in Step 5.

Add the
dummy spindles.
Place the posts
on the marks and
drill pilot holes for
their fasteners.
Secure the posts
to the board.

What's their story?
FAUCET HANDLES

Bathroom technology was pretty much perfected in the late 19th century. So why'd we have to mess with it? Case in point: the porcelain cross-style faucet handle. To crank up the heat—and water pressure—in your shower, you just turned the handle marked HOT. These days, it can require a manual to navigate high-tech digital control panels.

Luckily for Luddites like me, those old-timey handles were built to last and still grace many a well-preserved bathroom. Their debut coincided with the widespread use of compression faucets, which gave bathers variable control over water flow with the twist of a handle. Earlier ball-valve faucets relied on beer-tap-like levers that had just two settings: ON or OFF.

Compression faucets remain the most popular and easiest to maintain—great news for fans of the old cross-handles.

Glue on the escutcheons.

Mix a two-part fast-drying epoxy formulated for bonding metal. Spread the epoxy on the rims of the porcelain escutcheons and place them over the spindles.

Adhere the handle "hooks."

Fill the metal fittings at the base of each handle with epoxy and fit them on top of the spindles. Wipe away any epoxy that seeps out, and wait 5 minutes for the adhesive to set. (It takes 1 hour for it to cure.)

Put on the shelf.

Rest the shelf top on the brackets. To secure it in place, drill pilot holes and drive trim-head screws through the back of the mounting board and into the edge of the shelf. Now pick a nice spot in the bath for your new towel rack.

USE A

COTTAGE DOOR

TO MAKE A

Dressing Vanity

This sweet stand-up vanity made from a Victorian-era cottage door was inspired by a mirrored coat tree in the hallway of the 1890s house I grew up in. I use it for hanging hats and scarves in my bedroom, but you could just as easily prop it against a wall in a bathroom or in an entry, where it could function just like the tree it was patterned after. • Similar to an old window, the glass in a cottage door is typically cased in wood, with a sill comprising a protruding stool and apron molding underneath it. I made the stool a little deeper to create a sturdy shelf for holding grooming supplies and my morning coffee. Then I filled the empty space above the shelf with a new $70 mirror instead of replacement glass for the window that had shattered long ago. • My unrestored door, which was rescued from a ramshackle shotgun cottage in New Orleans, cost $350—a savings of about $300 over pristine, ready-to-install models. I covered holes, where two dead bolts once pierced the wood, with robe hooks I got on sale at a furniture store for just $5 apiece. Two more hooks on the opposite side add symmetry and provide more places to sling stuff. • A stylish primp spot like this makes getting ready in the morning—even on those hurry-up-and-rush-out-of-the-house days—a pleasant experience.

Supplies
COTTAGE DOOR
AND MATCHING WOOD
FOR THE SHELF
MIRROR GLASS
¼-INCH LAUAN PLYWOOD
4 ROBE HOOKS
PENCIL
SANDPAPER
WOOD GLUE
3-INCH TRIM-HEAD SCREWS
4-INCH DECK SCREWS
4D FINISHING NAILS
SILICONE ADHESIVE
FOR MIRROR

Tools
PRY BAR
PLIERS
JIGSAW
BLOCK PLANE
PAINTBRUSH
DRILL/DRIVER
¹⁄₁₆-INCH DRILL BIT
CAULK GUN
SCREWDRIVER

 7 HOURS   ABOUT $440   SKILL LEVEL: <u>DIFFICULT</u>

HOW-TO ➤

Start Here

Prep the mirror opening.
Start by removing the narrow window-stop moldings on the back side of the cottage door, using a small pry bar. Use pliers to pry out the old nails, and set the moldings aside.

Remove the stool and apron. Flip the door faceup and pry off the projecting ledge, or stool, and the decorative strip, or apron, below it. To prevent the wood from splitting, first loosen a corner. Then work down the molding's length with your pry bar, gently rocking the tool as you go. Set the moldings aside, and stand the door against a wall.

3 **4** **5** **6**

Set the stool on top of a new board.

Trace the outline of the stool's back edge on a board that's been cut to the same length. This is the board you'll use for the shelf, so choose one that closely matches the stool's thickness and the wood's patina. Mine is a cypress rail scavenged from another old door.

Determine where to notch the board.

Steady the board with its opposite, unmarked edge flush against the door where the stool used to sit. Mark where to notch the corners so that the board will fit snugly in the window frame once it's installed.

Cut along the pencil lines.

Use a jigsaw to create the notches. The board and stool should now fit together like puzzle pieces and slide easily into the door's window frame. To match the eased contours of the stool, plane and sand the sides of the newly cut board.

Create the shelf.

Join the stool and board by brushing both pieces with wood glue. Press them together, and drive 3-inch trim-head screws through the front of the stool. Be sure to first drill pilot holes, and to sink the screw heads below the surface.

Steps 7-10

**SEE
HOW IT'S
DONE**
View a
step-by-step
video for this
dressing vanity
project at
thisoldhouse
.com/books

7

8

9

Install the shelf.
Drill pilot holes,
and drive in 4-inch
screws, anchoring
them in the wood on
which the shelf sits.
Replace the apron
molding, securing
it with finishing
nails. To hide joinery
seams and screw
holes, use a filler
made of wood glue
and sawdust from
this project. Blend
until the mixture
is the consistency
of peanut butter.

**Apply mirror
adhesive.**
Return the door
to the worktable,
back side up.
Squeeze silicone
adhesive onto
the back of the
front window-stop
moldings.

Insert the mirror.
Carefully ease the
glass into place,
reflective side down.
Fit a sheet of lauan
plywood on the back
of the mirror, and
reattach the back
window-stop moldings
with finishing nails.

FINISHING TOUCH

*If you're like me and love the look
of bare wood, preserve it with a
PASTE WAX sealer. Choose a light-
brown color to warm up the wood
and bring out the grain. Just be
sure to first smooth the surface with
fine-grit sandpaper.*

Add the hooks.
Start by screwing the robe hooks' mounting plates to the door (a). If covering an existing hole, plug it first with a wood scrap that's glued in place. Now secure the hooks to the backplates (b), stand up the door, and commence grooming.

What's their story?

WINDOWED COTTAGE DOORS

The cottage door was the people's door. A door for the regular Joe, "the bone and sinew of the land." (That last one comes from the writings of the snooty yet influential 19th-century tastemaker A.J. Downing.) Metaphors aside, the cottage door was indeed designed for America's working class. Constructed of wood stiles and rails, with entry-brightening glass in the upper portion and carved moldings and decorative appliqués in the lower, it dressed up the exteriors of the most modest Italianate, Queen Anne, and Stick houses of the late 1800s.

Cottage doors still hang in front entries nationwide, but my money's on New Orleans for having the most per square mile. That's where durable cypress doors decorate the facades of thousands of shotgun cottages—and salvage yards are chock-full of the castoffs.

USE

CAST-IRON TUB FEET

TO MAKE AN

Umbrella Stand

Supplies

3 BATHTUB FEET
FLOWER BUCKET
¾-INCH PLYWOOD
PENCIL
SAFETY GLASSES
1½-INCH MACHINE SCREWS (¼-20) WITH WASHERS AND NUTS
DUCT TAPE
WHITE LATEX PAINT
WATER-BASED POLYURETHANE
LINT-FREE CLOTH

Tools

RULER
COMPASS
JIGSAW
CLAMPS
DRILL/DRIVER
¼-INCH DRILL BIT
RATCHET WRENCH
PAINTBRUSH

They're small, they're orphans, and they're usually quite dirty. Still, iron bathtub feet that have been separated from the rolled-top soakers they used to support are among the star attractions at salvage yards. It's no wonder, really, with their intricate castings of lion paws with drawn claws and eagle talons gripping balls. The feet typically date to the late 1800s or early 1900s, and cost from $10 to $25 each, depending on size and ornamentation. • Claw-foot tub interiors were coated in porcelain, but the outsides and feet were usually bare metal and periodically required a fresh coat of paint to prevent rust. White paint was the norm, but you can also find feet with a colored or even metallic finish. • When shopping for three matching feet to use as decorative supports for an umbrella stand, I had a silvery, painted patina in mind. I wanted to mount them to the base of a $12 galvanized-tin flower bucket and tie in with the metal, but also to add a little extra shimmer for a nice pick-me-up when it's dark and stormy outside.

 2 HOURS   ABOUT $70    SKILL LEVEL: <u>EASY</u>

HOW-TO

1

Make a plywood mounting board.
Using a ruler and compass, measure the diameter of the bucket's bottom, and draw a circle on the ¾-inch plywood that's 1 to 2 inches smaller than the bottom. Use a jigsaw to cut out the disk. This will be fixed to the bottom of the bucket to provide a stable mounting surface for the tub feet.

2

Drill mounting holes in the feet.
Clamp the feet to your worktable or in a vise (shown), and drill holes through the iron brackets that extend from the backs of the feet.

3

Mark locations for the feet.
Trace the outline of each foot's bracket on the wood disk, and mark for its screw holes. Set the disk on your worktable, and drill all three holes.

4   **5**   **6**

Add fasteners.
Place the wood disk on
the bucket's bottom,
and mark where to drill
corresponding holes.
Remove the disk, bore
holes, and insert 1½-inch
machine screws with
washers through the
inside of the bucket.
Hold the screwheads in
place with duct tape.

Secure the mounting disk and tub feet.
Fit the disk over the screws. Add the feet, using the
tracings on the wood as a guide to make sure each foot
is properly aligned. Loosely twist nuts onto the screws,
remove the duct tape covering the screwheads, and
tighten the assembly with a ratchet wrench.

**Give the bucket
instant patina.**
Brush on a wash that's
1 part white latex paint
to 3 parts polyurethane.
Dab with a lint-free cloth
until you achieve the look
you want. Let dry, and
place your new umbrella
stand by the front door
so that it's ready for use
on the first rainy day.

What's their story?
CAST-IRON TUB FEET

Designs for bathtub feet, which were used to elevate the vessels and give them a furniture-like look, were most
elaborate in the 1890s—the peak of the Victorian era. That's when Americans craved embellishment on even
the most utilitarian household objects. These ball-and-claw feet had wide "ankles" decorated with flowers, vines,
or shells that wrapped the base of the tub like shields. They were quite large—about 5 inches wide by 7 inches
tall—and weighed 4 or 5 pounds each. By the early 1930s, when the popularity of claw-foot tubs began to fade,
feet were often small unadorned balls supported by smooth ankles.

USE

A FIREPLACE SUMMER FRONT

TO MAKE A

Supplies

FIREPLACE SUMMER FRONT
2×4 HARDWOOD BOARD
1½-INCH ANGLE-IRON STRIPS
WORK GLOVES
N100 DUST MASK
CLEAR SPRAY SEALER
SAFETY GLASSES
PENCIL
¼-BY-2-INCH HEX BOLTS WITH WASHERS AND NUTS

Tools

WIRE BRUSH
TAPE MEASURE
JIGSAW
SAW BLADES FOR WOOD AND METAL
CLAMPS
RULER
DRILL/DRIVER
⁵⁄₁₆-INCH COBALT DRILL BIT
STEEL PUNCH
HAMMER
RATCHET WRENCH

Log Rack

For an adaptation project that plays off the original function of a fireplace summer front—as a decorative cover to seal off the hearth during warm months—turn it into a log storage rack. That way, you can admire the intricate detailing in the sturdy metal panel even in the winter, when you're cozied up in front of a toasty fire. • Summer fronts typically cost around $165 for a cast-iron Victorian-era model with a lacy floral design, like mine, or a solid-tin panel from the early 1900s that's stamped with a geometric pattern. Expect to pay more for panels that are cast or stamped with elaborate designs, such as pastoral scenes, animals, or cameo-like profiles. • To make a log rack, you'll also need a hardwood board (about 4½ feet long) that you can cut to form rails for the bottom, and an L-shaped steel angle-iron strip (5 feet should do it) to use for the vertical back supports. • Rather than bust out a blowtorch, my friend Jennifer and I joined all the parts with hefty nuts and bolts. The result is a stylish and sturdy storage piece that cradles a lot more logs than a common home-center holder.

 3 HOURS $180   SKILL LEVEL: <u>DIFFICULT</u>

HOW-TO ➤

Start Here

Clean the metal.

Pull on work gloves, and use a wire brush to knock off rusty high spots on your summer front. Be sure to wet the surface first and wear an N100 dust mask to guard against lead.

Protect the finish.

Prop up the summer front, and spray on a rust-inhibiting clear sealer to prevent any future corrosion. My two-piece summer front still had its detachable surround (sometimes these get left behind when old buildings are dismantled). I put the decorative center panel aside and reattached it after the rest of the log rack was complete.

Don't forget...

When gathering your gear at the home center, be sure to grab a fresh jigsaw blade and a drill bit designed specifically for sawing and boring through metal. Trust me, I quickly blew through two old bits putting holes in this cast-iron front.

3

4

5

Measure and cut the rack's wood rails.
Mark the desired length of the holder—mine is 21 inches—on two 2×4 hardwood boards. Use a jigsaw to cut the boards, which will serve as the bottom rails. Cut a third rail to the width of the summer front to use as the rack's horizontal back support.

Cut the angle irons.
For the vertical back supports, measure the height of the summer front and mark the length on a pair of 1½-inch angle irons. Clamp the angles to your worktable, and cut them with your jigsaw. Cut a second pair of 6-inch angles to fasten to the front itself.

Mark where the fasteners will go.
Indicate where the bolts will attach the angle irons to both the summer front and the wood rails. Center marks at ¾ inch and 2 inches from the bottom end. Then flip the angle, and mark the same measurements at the top of the angle's opposing side.

Steps 6-10

6

Bore holes in the angle irons. Fit your drill/driver with a $5/16$-inch cobalt bit to create the holes for the two ¼-inch bolts in all four angle irons. To prevent your bit from moving when you drill, first make an indentation by steadying a steel punch on the mark and tapping it with a hammer.

What's their story?
FIREPLACE SUMMER FRONTS

When summer fronts were first made, in the mid- to late 1800s, homeowners relied on fireplaces fueled by wood or coal to heat their homes. In warm seasons, when the fireplace wasn't in use, they would cover the opening so as not to see an ashy pit. Come winter, they'd simply remove it and spark up a fire.

That changed in the thermostat age. Today, the fronts are often left in place year-round on nonworking fireplaces that have been sealed off to prevent a home's cooled or warmed air from escaping up the chimney. In this case, the filigreed or figural fronts offer a decorative way to conceal the brickwork used to fill in the firebox.

7

8

9

10

Secure the short angle irons.
Position the 6-inch pieces vertically on the back of the summer front, and use the punch to mark where the bolts will go. Drill corresponding holes in the summer front, insert the bolts and washers, and twist on the nuts.

Bore holes in the wood rails.
Mark on the bottom wood rails and on the horizontal back support where they'll be joined with the angle irons. Drill for the bolt holes.

Secure the rails.
Align the holes in the bottom wood rails with those in the angle irons attached to the summer front. Insert the bolts, cap with washers, and twist on the nuts. Next, secure the long angle irons to the rear ends of the wood rails.

Finish by adding the back support.
Fit the horizontal board between the rear angle irons at their tops, and secure the pieces with bolts. Your rack is now ready to be stacked with logs.

SEE HOW IT'S DONE
View a step-by-step video for this log-rack project at
thisoldhouse.com/books

USE

STAIR SPINDLES

TO MAKE A

Console Table

My friend David came to me with a problem: How to create a central repository for keys, dog leashes, and mail in his tiny front entry without gobbling up precious square footage? Easy. Build a two-legged console that saves space by anchoring directly to the wall. • To match the lived-in look of his farmhouse, we built the table ourselves using salvaged stair parts. For the front legs, we chose a pair of green-painted spindles we found at a New York City salvage yard for $50 (high prices come with the territory, but you can get them online for as little as $14 a pair). The top is an old heart-pine stair tread, 11 inches deep and 36 inches long, that we got for $15. And to replicate the look of a stair's vertical riser—salvage yards usually don't stock these—we cut a $5 rough-sawn pine board for the console table's apron-style front and sides, using a standard 7½-inch height. • Now installed in the entry, the console helps David control clutter while also providing a playful connection with the home's staircase, which originates in the room.

Supplies
2 WOOD SPINDLES
STAIR TREAD
ROUGH-SAWN BOARD
OR STAIR RISER
PENCIL
2×4 FOR BLOCKING
2-INCH DECK SCREWS

Tools
TONGUE-AND-GROOVE
PLIERS
SCRAPER
SPEED SQUARE
JIGSAW
CLAMPS
DRILL/DRIVER
COUNTERSINK COMBO BIT
LEVEL

3 HOURS $70   SKILL LEVEL: <u>MODERATE</u>

HOW-TO

Start Here

Mark where to trim the tread. You'll need to remove any notches or unevenness on the ends. Use a Speed Square (shown) or combination square and a pencil to draw straight cut lines where the tread was originally attached to the stair framing.

Tidy up the tread.
Remove old fasteners (nails or carpet staples) from the stair tread with tongue-and-groove pliers. Use a scraper to remove any glue or paint residue.

3 **4** **5**

Steps 6-9

Trim the tread.
Cut along the lines
using a jigsaw.
To steady the tool,
clamp a wood
scrap to the tread
as a guide.

**Determine
the apron
boards' lengths.**
Flip the tread
over and draw
layout lines on the
underside, leaving
a ¾-inch reveal at
the front and sides.
Mark and cut the
apron boards to fit
within the lines.

**Mark where
blocking will go.**
Arrange the apron
boards on the
tread. Trace a line
along their inside
edges, where you'll
attach 2×4 interior
blocking onto which
you'll screw the
apron. Now mark
and cut the blocking
to fit within the lines.

TIP ☞ To remove nails without marring a
wood surface, I pull them from the back side
with pliers. Hammering nails back through
the face can cause the wood to splinter.

Create paths for the fasteners. Fit your drill/driver with a countersink combination bit and drill pilot holes through the blocking. You'll use 2-inch deck screws driven at an angle to secure the blocking to the tread. The same size screws will attach the blocking horizontally to the apron.

What's their story?
STAIR SPINDLES

The fancy newel post at the bottom of the stairs always gets the attention, but it's the spindles—those leggy beauties steadying the handrail—that do the heavy lifting.

Before the Industrial Revolution brought mechanical lathes to turn wood quickly and cheaply, these spindles were typically unadorned, save for those in the grand stair halls of the superwealthy. But by Victorian times, the plain little pickets had been transformed with decorative beading, graceful twists, and classical fluting details.

Millwork catalogs from the late 1800s showed dozens of spindle designs in various wood types. Builders often picked pine, which they painted so that the spindles would match the stair's vertical risers or other trim in the room.

7 8 9

Fasten the parts together.

Clamp the blocking in place, and drive the screws into the tread at an angle. Next, wrap the apron boards around the blocking, secure with clamps, and drive in the screws horizontally.

Add the spindle "legs."

Secure the spindles to the apron's front and sides using 2-inch screws. Drill countersink pilot holes first, to recess the screws and prevent the wood from splitting.

Secure the console to the wall.

Cut a wood strip that fits between the console table's interior blocking. Mount the strip level on the wall at the height of the table's underside, using fasteners and anchors appropriate for your wall type. Rest the table on the strip, and join the two with screws driven at an angle through the strip and into the underside of the tabletop. Be sure to first drill pilot holes. Now start using your new entryway catchall—and finally stop losing your keys.

USE

A CHIMNEY POT

TO MAKE A

Landscape Light

Among the simplest creative reuse projects I've done, this chimney-pot-turned-garden-light is also one of my favorites. That's partly because I love proving naysayers wrong. • Most of my friends couldn't visualize a chimney pot, much less a chimney pot that could cast a warm glow on the underside of a Japanese maple tree's canopy. I admit the name does sound like some sort of medieval cauldron for boiling the sneaky squirrels that build nests in your chimney. But the "pots" are actually terra-cotta cylinders that sit atop stacks to help improve fireplace draw. • I finally found a believer in an outdoor lighting pro, who not only dug the idea but helped me figure out all the parts for the project. First on the shopping list is the chimney pot—I got one with a crown-shaped top at a New Jersey salvage yard for $200. Next is a low-voltage well light to fit inside the pot's base, and a transformer that plugs directly into an all-weather outlet to power the light. Expect to pay about $100 for both. • Be sure to choose a transformer with a built-in timer that automatically turns the light on and off each night after a few hours. That way you save yourself from having to remember to flip the switch while also saving energy by not leaving the light on when you aren't around, or awake, to enjoy it.

Supplies
VINTAGE CHIMNEY POT
50-WATT WELL LIGHT
TRANSFORMER
METAL MESH
LEATHER WORK GLOVES

Tools
WIRE STRIPPER
SNIPS
SHOVEL

 2 HOURS $300 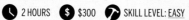 SKILL LEVEL: <u>EASY</u>

HOW-TO ▶▶

Start Here

Hook up the transformer.
Strip ½ inch of plastic insulation from the ends of the light cord, and slip the exposed copper wires into the transformer's corresponding terminals.

Make a leaf guard.
Use snips to cut metal mesh, such as scrap hardware cloth (shown) or an old window screen, to the diameter of the chimney pot's top opening.

Insert the guard.
Pull on work gloves and fold the edges of the metal mesh so that it fits snugly in the opening. The guard will keep leaves from gathering inside the pot and blocking the light source.

4

5

6

▶

**SEE
HOW IT'S
DONE**
View a
step-by-step
video for this
chimney pot
landscape light
project at
**thisoldhouse
.com/books**

Dig a trench.
Once you've
established a spot for
your light, use a shovel
to excavate a 6-inch-
deep trench for the
low-voltage well light
and the transformer's
cord to sit in.

Install the light.
Place the light and
cord in the trench,
then backfill with
the loose soil or use
gravel to promote
drainage. Leave the bulb
exposed, but be sure
to completely bury the
cord to protect it.

Lift the chimney
pot into place.
Position it so that the
light is centered in the
pot's base. Plug in the
transformer, and set
the timer so that the
light will glow for a
few hours every night,
starting at dusk.

What's their story?
CHIMNEY POTS

Shaped like the rooks in a chess set, with tapered bodies and vented, crown-like tops, chimney pots have protruded from European rooftops for centuries. You might recall that Mary Poppins—held aloft by her umbrella—famously glided among London's antique pots.

In America, they were mainly used from the late 1800s to the early 1900s, when people burned coal to heat their homes. Mortared to the top of a masonry chimney, the terra-cotta pot was an inexpensive way to extend the stack height and increase draw, reducing the amount of soot and fumes that entered living spaces. Chimney pots were also used to accentuate the houses' architecture. Nearly every design in A.J. Downing's influential 1850 pattern book, *The Architecture of Country Houses*, is crowned by at least one.

SALVAGE STAR

★ LYNN BOUGHTON
BROOKLYN, MI
/ STREET SCORE SLEUTH /

Look what one This Old House reader did!

"MY RECYCLED GARDEN RETREAT"

When *TOH* reader Lynn Boughton moved into her home, the shed out back hadn't been used in years. "It was essentially a condominium for chipmunks," says Lynn. But with some work, she knew the building could be a focal point in the new hosta garden she was planning. Now, with its walls of salvaged windows, winding front path, and welcoming front porch, Lynn's remodeled shed hosts her visiting family and friends, not trespassing critters.

1. GARDEN SHED Lynn was able to preserve the existing shed by shoring up shaky walls and enlarging and reframing the window openings. Inside, she removed a dropped ceiling to reveal the roof trusses; a swinging daybed now hangs from one. Lynn covered the underside of the roof sheathing with pine tongue-and-groove flooring she got at a garage sale for $50 a truckload.

2. STEPPING STONES Lynn found the reclaimed sandstone pavers that lead to the shed's new front porch piled up at the end of a neighbor's driveway. "Instead having stuff hauled away, people in my town just put it out because they know treasure hunters like me will take it."

3. CASEMENT WINDOWS The key to turning the dark little shed into a light-filled lounge was windows, and lots of 'em, says Lynn. But she worried she wouldn't find enough matching vintage ones to make an impact. Then she got lucky. "Driving along one day I came across a guy who was replacing all the wavy-glass casement windows in his 1920s Craftsman cottage. He just let me take them for free!"

USE

A MEDICINE CABINET

TO MAKE A

Message Center

Supplies
MEDICINE CABINET
WOOD PUTTY
SANDPAPER
PAINTER'S TAPE
LATEX PRIMER
DISPOSABLE PLASTIC
CONTAINER
CORK TILES
WOOD GLUE
CHALKBOARD PAINT
MAGNETIC DOOR CATCH
CUP HOOKS
DOOR PULL
CHALK

Tools
PAINTBRUSH
UTILITY KNIFE
STEEL RULER
SMALL FOAM ROLLER
SCREWDRIVER
DRILL/DRIVER
1/16-INCH DRILL BIT

Tired of littering my countertop with house keys, bills, and various daily reminders to my husband and babysitter, I set out in search of a medicine cabinet to transform into an organizer for a corner of the kitchen. • A scan of the online classifieds turned up a gorgeous wall-mount oak model with a combination of shelves and cubbies inside for just $65—a bargain because it was missing its mirror—and perfect for what I had planned. Rather than fill the empty recess on the face of the cabinet door with new glass, I brushed on chalkboard paint, which you can find at home centers for about $12 per quart. I lined the inside of the door with 12-by-12-inch cork tiles that I got at a crafts store ($7 for a four-pack). And added a tidy row of 25-cent cup hooks, screwed into the underside of the medicine cabinet's top ledge, that's just right for hanging keys. • Now that I've got my handy message center, there's no more scribbling on scraps of paper. When I want to bark out an order or two, I just write it on the chalkboard.

 2 HOURS $90 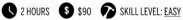 SKILL LEVEL: <u>EASY</u>

HOW-TO ➡

Start Here

Fix cracks
or gouges.
Fill damaged areas
in the cabinet
door's recessed
front panel with
wood putty.
Let dry, then
sand smooth.

Tape around the front recess.
Use blue painter's tape to protect the panel's surrounding
stile-and-rail frame from errant brushstrokes when applying
primer and chalkboard paint.

3 **4** **5** **6**

Prime the front recess.
Brush on a latex primer so that the chalkboard paint will adhere properly. Rather than dipping your brush directly into the paint can, pour a small amount into a disposable plastic container and work from that.

Cut the cork.
While you wait for the primer to dry, open the cabinet door and trim two 12-by-12-inch cork tiles to fit within the recess on its interior side. A few passes with a utility knife steadied against a steel ruler will ensure crisp edges.

Adhere the cork.
Squeeze wood glue onto the back side of the cork sheets, and press them into place. The glue typically bonds within 30 minutes.

Apply the chalkboard paint.
Close the door and use a small foam roller to evenly spread the low-odor latex chalkboard paint over the primer. It dries to the touch in 20 minutes and is ready for a second coat in 4 hours.

Steps 7-10

Add a magnetic catch. Screw the magnet component to the cabinet's inner side wall. Align and secure the metal strike plate on the door. (Skip this step if your cabinet has an operable latch.)

What's their story?
MEDICINE CABINETS

Vintage over-the-sink cabinets work just as well to store modern mousse as they did old-timey hair tonics back in the day. And, in varied designs from Art Deco ones with flower-etched mirrors to Craftsman models with chunky cupboard latches, they've also got style.

Wall-hung cabinets tend to be older, some dating to the mid-1800s, and are typically made of wood. Recessed ones that fit between the studs were made of wood or metal. These became popular in the late 1800s, in part because of the Victorians' obsession with cleanliness. It was thought that protruding ledges, specifically those in kitchens and bathrooms, harbored icky microbes. These days, the recessed ones are prized as space-savers.

8 **9** **10**

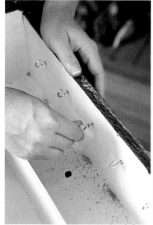

Screw in cup hooks.
For dense hardwood cabinets like my oak one, use a drill/driver to bore a line of pilot holes into the underside of the cabinet's top. Then twist in the hooks to serve as key hangers.

Add a door pull.
Position a knob over the existing hole where the old door hardware used to be, and secure the pull from behind with a screw. (Skip this step if your cabinet still has its original pull.)

Condition the blackboard.
Wait three days for the paint to cure, then prepare the board for use by rubbing the side of a piece of chalk over the entire surface and erasing. Once you've got a clean slate, christen it with a message.

Embrace flaws
DON'T GO CRAZY REPAIRING EVERY NICK IN OLD WOOD. IT'S THE LITTLE BLEMISHES THAT ADD CHARACTER.

USE

A FACADE FRAGMENT

TO MAKE A

Tool Holder

The deep ledge on this terra-cotta cornice with a classical egg-and-dart motif made it ideal for the top shelf of a garden-tool rack I wanted to build for a green-thumbed friend. The 19-inch-long facade fragment, which had been part of decorative banding beneath a roof's eaves, was rescued from a demolished early-20th-century building in New York City. • Fortunately, when ornately adorned homes, businesses, and public institutions come down, there are oftentimes recyclers with the sense to spare exterior stone or terra-cotta details, such as the fluted pilasters that flank doors, and the chunky keystones centered in lintel moldings above windows. Case in point: the local salvage dealer who sold me my $75 cornice section. And, of course, my coworkers at *TOH*, who rarely trash anything. For the wood base of my rack, I scrounged around in our editorial closet, where we store props for photo shoots, and found just the thing: a beat-up beam with the carpenter's saw marks still visible on one side. I wasn't so lucky with the hooks for hanging the garden tools. After searching in vain at three different salvage yards for five matching wrought-iron ones, I resorted to reproduction cut-nail hooks from an online hardware shop that I got for about $5 each. • Now, with all my parts assembled, all I had to do was wait for the next sunny day to start building—and getting my friend ready to pot her blooms in style.

Supplies
TERRA-COTTA CORNICE
WOOD BOARD
WROUGHT-IRON HOOKS
POLYURETHANE
CONSTRUCTION ADHESIVE
L-SHAPED BRACKETS
PENCIL

Tools
CAULK GUN
CLAMP
DRILL/DRIVER
1/16-INCH DRILL BIT
COMBINATION SQUARE
LEVEL

2 HOURS   ABOUT $100   SKILL LEVEL: <u>EASY</u>

HOW-TO ➤

Start Here

Attach the board to the cornice.
Squeeze polyurethane construction adhesive on the underside of the cornice and on the top of the board. Adhere the parts and secure with a clamp until the glue dries.

Reinforce the bond with brackets.
Glue one leg of each L-shaped bracket inside a recess in the rear of the cornice. Drill pilot holes, and attach the other leg to the board with the screws provided. Remove the clamp.

Map out hook locations.
Use a combination square and pencil to measure and mark on the board where the five hooks go. Space them an equal distance from each other and from the bottom of the cornice.

4

5

6

7

Drill
pilot holes.
Position your
drill/driver's bit
on the pencil
marks, and bore
holes for the
hooks' supplied
fasteners.

Secure
the hooks.
Align the
hardware over
the holes and
use the drill/driver
to screw in
the fasteners.

Mark where to
hang the holder.
Draw a level line
where you'll secure
it to the wall. Steady
a torpedo level on a
wood strip (shown)
or use a 2-foot level.

Install the holder.
Drill pilot holes
in the board for the
mounting screws.
Steady the holder
on the line, and fasten
it to the wall. The
holder may be heavy,
so use screws long
enough to anchor
it to wall framing.

What's their story?
FACADE FRAGMENTS

In Rome, the cleaved columns, fractured friezes, and other rock-like ruins of ancient civilizations are strewn about tourist destinations for folks to touch and admire. Here in the States, we tend to keep architectural artifacts under lock and key, or at least under the watchful eye of a museum guard.

Luckily, though, there are fragments of somewhat recent vintage at salvage yards that you can not only handle but also buy and bring home. What you'll find are stone pieces from the 1800s that were hand-carved by European immigrants, as well as terra-cotta decorations, such as my cornice from around 1910. The latter, which came bare—in earthy red or white—or coated in colorful glazes, were popular because they could be mass-produced from molds.

USE

WOOD DOOR CASING

TO MAKE A

Pier Mirror

The public rooms of houses where Victorians welcomed and entertained their guests were often decorated with large pier mirrors. Before electric lighting, mirrors served a purpose we don't usually think of: brightening interior spaces. Installed between windows in front parlors, tall pier mirrors reflected natural light. • Today, a pier mirror is a welcome addition almost anywhere in the house. My mom—a serial renovator—had a beautiful gilded version that she carted from one old-house project to the next, propping it against a foyer wall or in a bedroom to serve as a dressing mirror. • For my DIY pier mirror, I used the ornately carved wood entablature of an old door casing for the top; I got it for $200 at an antiques shop. The sides and bottom, which are joined with plinth blocks, are made from preprimed pine pilasters, and the frame's back is plywood. I had the parts, which totaled $150, cut to size at the lumberyard. The 3-by-6-foot mirror was a custom order from a glass shop for $160. • To unify the old door casing with the new wood, I brushed the frame with gloss white paint for a lacquered look. Now it's not just the mirror that sparkles—the frame has a shiny, light-reflective quality too.

6+ HOURS $510 SKILL LEVEL: DIFFICULT

HOW-TO ➤

Start Here

Dry-fit the parts.
Arrange the pre-cut pilaster frame around the mirror. Lay a 2× board that's slightly thicker than the rest of the frame's parts across the top to support the entablature. My entablature had mitered corners that used to wrap the sides of the door casing, so I sized the 2× board to match the width of its back.

Assemble the mirror frame.
Join the pilasters to the plinths by driving in pocket-hole screws on the diagonal along the backs of the wood. Use your drill/driver and a pocket-hole jig to bore the holes. Then join the 2× top to the pilaster's ends.

3 **4** **5**

Apply glue to the frame's back.
Use a caulk gun to squeeze a bead of construction adhesive along the back.

Secure the plywood back to the frame.
Adhere the panel. Drive 1-inch deck screws into the four corners and every 8 inches along the top, sides, and bottom of the back panel.

Adhere the entablature.
Flip the frame faceup, and use the construction adhesive to affix the decorative entablature to the 2× top. Secure with clamps.

➤➜
Steps 6-8

Tool School

I got my DIY-friendly POCKET-HOLE JIG—long used by pros to secure frame corners—at a home center. Basically, if you can use a drill, you can make perfect joints with this handy jig, which makes angled holes for joining boards with screws.

▶

**SEE
HOW IT'S
DONE.**
View a
step-by-step
video for this
pier mirror
project at
**thisoldhouse
.com/books**

6

7

Complete the entablature top.

Flip the frame
facedown again,
and reinforce the
glue by driving
2-inch deck screws
through the back
of the 2× board.
If your entablature
has mitered
corners, secure
them with wood
glue so that
they wrap the
board's ends.

Paint the frame.

Brush on an oil-based enamel to give the piece a lacquer-like
finish. Be sure to first prime the entablature top if it has
been stripped of its old paint or has been stained,
as mine was. Sand between coats.

Add the mirror glass and bead molding.
Adhere the mirror, using special glue called mirror mastic. Enlist a friend to help ease the glass in place. Cover its edges with bead molding affixed to the frame with wood glue. Now stand the mirror where it'll brighten both the room and your mood.

What's their story?
WOOD DOOR CASINGS

Judging by the door casings shown above, the houses they came from were quite grand. The floral and fan details in the entablature tops were seen in the door surrounds of Victorian-era houses from the late 1800s. Their heights—about 12 feet—indicate that the casings were used on the first floor, where ceilings were lofty and houseguests would be sure to see them.

By the turn of the 20th century, door casings reflected a less fussy Arts and Crafts aesthetic that prized natural wood grain and clean lines. The lower ceilings in Craftsman bungalows also left less room for those fancy entablature tops, which were made by stacking up to six moldings to form one big one.

These days, salvage yards are one of the best sources for wood door casings, which can be reused in new houses and in period restorations, making drab doorways with thin or nonexistent surrounds more attractive.

USE

METAL CEILING TILES

TO MAKE A

Planter Box

The patterns on old metal ceilings were stamped in a tic-tac-toe formation, but instead of X's and O's, the same floral or geometric design was repeated in each quadrant. In the late 1800s, you could pick up these decorative ceiling "tiles" for just 10 cents per square foot. Today, vintage originals sell at salvage yards for $3 to $20 per square foot, depending on how fanciful their design and the condition they're in. • For my tin planter box project, I used a reclaimed tiled panel with a grid of four 6-by-6-inch squares stacked one on top of the other and 12 across. Working from those dimensions, I cut wood sides for the box and neatly folded the metal around the four corners. I left 6 inches of extra material at the top so that I could tuck the last layer of metal squares inside the box for a finished look. • To guard against rot and insects, I built the box out of ½-inch pressure-treated plywood and inserted a $10 plastic planter to cradle the soil and blooms. The lightweight, removable liner also makes it easier to switch out plantings as seasons change.

Supplies
METAL CEILING TILES
½-INCH PRESSURE-TREATED PLYWOOD
N100 DUST MASK
LEATHER WORK GLOVES
SAFETY GLASSES
1½-INCH SIDING NAILS
1-INCH ROOFING NAILS
PLASTIC PLANTER LINER

Tools
WIRE BRUSH
HAMMER OR NAIL GUN (OPTIONAL)
STRAIGHT-CUT SNIPS
RUBBER MALLET

 2 HOURS   ABOUT $60    SKILL LEVEL: <u>MODERATE</u>

HOW-TO ➤

Start Here

Clean the metal.
Use a wire brush to remove loose rust and cracked paint. To guard against lead, which can be released in paint dust, work outdoors, wet the brush, and wear an N100 dust mask. Be sure to pull on leather work gloves to prevent your hands from getting cut on the metal.

Build the box.
Cut and fasten together 18-by-18-inch panels of pressure-treated plywood to form the sides of the planter box. I used a nail gun, but a hammer and 1½-inch siding nails also work just fine.

Create a base for the box.
Secure the bottom. I used a 16-by-16-inch panel, sliced in two, leaving a 2-inch gap in the middle for water to drain through. To help reinforce the box and raise it off the ground, cut a pair of scrap lumber "feet" to the length of the box. Nail these perpendicular to the bottom boards.

4

5

Steps 6-9

Wrap the box.
Fold the metal
sheet around the
sides of the planter,
and use a rubber
mallet to tap it flush
against the wood.

Cut the metal to size.
Use straight-cut snips to create a 24-by-73-inch sheet to sheath
the plywood box. It should have four 6-by-6-inch patterned
squares stacked one on top of the other and 12 across, plus an
extra inch in the length so that the edges can overlap.

TIP ☞ When using snips, fully open the
jaws but only partially close them to make
continuous cuts. Snapping the jaws shut
can crimp the metal's edges, leaving sharp points.

▶

**SEE
HOW IT'S
DONE**
View a
step-by-step
video for this
tin-wrapped
planter-box
project at
thisoldhouse
.com/books

6

7

8

**Secure
the metal.**
Fasten the tile
sheet to the
planter box by
hammering in
1-inch galvanized
roofing nails
along the sheet's
bottom seam.

**Cut the metal
corners.**
Use snips to cut
the corners where
the tile sheet
overlaps the top
of the planter.

Cover the edges.
Fold the extra row
of tiles over the
planter's top edge;
tap flush against
the inner walls. To
preserve the metal's
aged patina and
prevent more rust,
apply an exterior
polyurethane or
spray-on lacquer.

➡ **GOOD TO KNOW**
"Tin ceiling" is a misnomer that some historians
attribute to a Victorian-era belief that mass-
produced metalwares were cheap and flimsy,
like tin. The tiles were actually quite sturdy,
made of zinc, iron, or steel.

9

Drop in the liner and fill the planter. Insert the plastic liner, and complete your planter project by adding soil and eye-catching flowers.

What's their story?
METAL CEILING TILES

As an affordable alternative to the pricey ornamental plaster used for centuries by wealthy Europeans, U.S. manufacturers in the 1880s began stamping garland, quatrefoil, and geometric motifs into sheet metal. Cut and shaped into tiles, cove moldings, and medallions, the pieces fit together in interlocking grids that could be nailed directly to wood strips secured to ceiling joists.

The easy-to-install tiles were popular among the fashion-conscious middle class because once painted white the embossed metal was almost indistinguishable from more expensive plaster details.

As metal manufacturing moved into munitions at the onset of World War II, the availability of embossed ceiling tiles and trim declined. Today, just a handful of companies stamp out new panels based on the old designs, but period originals are still plentiful at most salvage yards.

USE

METAL DOORKNOBS

TO MAKE A

Coatrack

Supplies
6 CAST-METAL DOORKNOBS
AND ROSETTE BACKPLATES
WOOD TRIM OR BOARD
6 DUMMY DOOR SPINDLES
PENCIL
DECORATIVE SCREWS
HOT-GLUE STICKS
BEESWAX POLISH
LINT-FREE CLOTH

Tools
COMBINATION SQUARE
DRILL/DRIVER
1/16-INCH DRILL BIT
SCREWDRIVER
HOT-GLUE GUN

At my house, coats pile up on dining room chairs and get put away only when dinner guests actually need to sit. I have a coat closet—two, in fact—but after a long day at work, I hate messing with hangers. So for a project using vintage cast-brass doorknobs, a toss-and-go coatrack seemed just the antidote for my lazy ways. • For the rack's "hooks," I bought a mixed lot of six knobs and their matching rosette backplates for $6 to $25 each from a Texas salvage yard; all I needed was a nice old board to mount them on. Rather than set off on another shopping expedition, I put out the word to a few fellow junker friends. Lucky for me, one of them was willing to part with some chestnut door trim that he'd rescued after taking down a wall in his house. It would cost $25 to $50 for a similar piece from a salvage yard. • Storage space allowing, we junkers save everything. Even when an old house part has outlived its original purpose, there's always a new use for it just waiting to be dreamed up.

 1–2 HOURS $ $100 SKILL LEVEL: EASY

HOW-TO ➤

Start Here

Determine the knob placement.

Using a pencil and a combination square, lightly draw a horizontal line across the center of the board, then put evenly spaced vertical lines through it to indicate where to mount each knob.

Secure the mounting posts.

Position a dummy spindle (a post that holds a stationary knob, available at home centers) over each crosshair marking, and attach with the screws provided. Be sure to first drill pilot holes, using a drill/ driver fitted with a $\frac{1}{16}$-inch bit.

Conceal the post bases.

Place your rosettes over the dummy spindles, drill pilot holes, and secure them to the board with decorative screws.

GOOD TO KNOW

To figure out a doorknob's age, check its back. Knobs made before 1890 often have patterns on both sides, while newer ones have designs only on the face. Old brass also tends to contain more copper, giving the knob a red cast.

4   **5**

Glue on the knobs.

Secure each of the knobs to a spindle using hot glue. Unlike permanent epoxy, this melted adhesive quickly holds tight when it cools but still allows you to remove the knobs in case you ever want to reinstall them on doors.

Protect the wood.

Apply a natural wood polish, such as one containing beeswax. Now hang your rack using the appropriate anchors for your wall type, and start tidying up your front entry hall.

What's their story?
CAST-METAL DOORKNOBS

Beginning in the mid-1800s, American foundries created elaborate cast-metal door-knobs to complement new Victorian-era houses.

These Second Empire, Stick, Eastlake, and Queen Anne styles were downright romantic, and deserving of doorknobs that were more expressive than the plain porcelain or pressed-glass ones used before.

During this golden age of doorknobs cast in brass, bronze, and iron, popular motifs included animals, monograms, flowers, ships, and geometric shapes, as well as symbols of fraternal organizations, state seals, and school insignias.

After the turn of the 20th century, you could still find quality castings, but foundries had begun replacing both workmen and artisans with machines. Simple knobs made of inexpensive pressed tin or metal alloys soon became the norm.

 SEE HOW IT'S DONE
View a step-by-step video for this doorknob coatrack project at thisoldhouse.com/books

SALVAGE STAR

★ SUSAN AND MARK NITCHMAN
ST. CHARLES, MO   / DIEHARD DIYERS /

Look what these This Old House *readers did!*

"OUR NEW, RECLAIMED BATH"

Rather than buying new fixtures and cabinetry for the bathroom addition to their Victorian-era Queen Anne, *TOH* readers Susan and Mark Nitchman freshened up salvaged ones and got to work in the woodshop. The goal: Stay under their $6,000 budget without sacrificing a single spa-like amenity, such as the soaker tub, marble tiles, and custom storage pieces.

1. GLASS-FRONT CABINETS The doors came from a display at a kitchen showroom. "They were just going to be trashed," says Mark, who built plywood cabinet boxes to match the doors' dimensions. The corbels beneath are pedestal wall shelves from a furniture store. Semigloss white latex paint unifies the cabinet parts.

2. CLASSIC CLAW-FOOT By saving money with a salvaged tub given to them by a friend—all it needed was new paint—the couple could splurge on a new chrome faucet. They used white, oil-based enamel on the tub sides, and silver on the feet.

3. DIY ÉTAGÈRE Mark crafted this unit almost entirely out of scavenged parts. The marble slab, an orphaned piece that once topped an antique table, was $1, and the pilasters with the button motif on the upper shelves were $5, at tag sales. The trim matches carving on the lower portion of the étagère—a piece the couple once used to corral kitchen gear.

USE

A KITCHEN SINK

TO MAKE AN

Outdoor Bar

For several weeks one summer my *TOH* coworker Hylah had been inviting me to her boyfriend's lakefront cottage. Sure, she enjoys my company. But she also wanted to build the outdoor bar that we'd designed together the previous winter, when dreaming of cocktails on the deck pulled us out of a February funk. • The core of the project is a 1950s cast-iron sink with an integral drain board that Hylah got at a salvage yard for $200, including the faucet. It's supported by a $279 cedar potting bench that we assembled in about an hour from a kit. • Stoppered and filled with ice, the sink basin is great for chilling beers and mixers. And when the party's over, you simply funnel waste water into a bucket placed below the sink or, if you use an adapter to attach the faucet to a garden hose, divert the waste through PVC piping hooked up beneath the drain. To hide the bottom storage shelf—great for stashing extra bags of chips, serving dishes, and even charcoal for your BBQ—Hylah stitched colorful curtains made from 4 yards of Sunbrella fabric she'd bought for $67. • Now, whenever she welcomes me back to the cottage, it's for margaritas, not manual labor. Those are the best invitations.

Supplies
CAST-IRON KITCHEN SINK
POTTING BENCH KIT
SUNBRELLA FABRIC
1½-INCH STAINLESS-STEEL SCREWS
PENCIL
SILICONE CAULK
PAINTER'S TAPE
½-INCH EYEBOLTS
⅜-INCH DOWELS

Tools
DRILL/DRIVER
TAPE MEASURE
FRAMING SQUARE
JIGSAW
CAULK GUN

 4 HOURS $ ABOUT $550   SKILL LEVEL: <u>MODERATE</u>

78

HOW-TO ➤

Start Here

1

2

Build the bench.
Assemble the kit, leaving off the upper shelf. Next, cut a piece of scrap wood to the length of the bench top and secure it to the back edge with stainless-steel screws. Coupled with additional scrap wood braces that link the strip to the bench's back legs, the assembly will give the bench extra strength to hold the heavy sink.

Measure the sink basin.
Take measurements on all four sides to calculate how big a hole to make in the bench top to accommodate the sink basin.

FINISHING TOUCH

The beauty of using cedar for outdoor furniture is that it's naturally rot resistant. But to keep the sun from turning its color from a warm honey to a drab gray, I like to apply a water-based **CLEAR WOOD SEALER** with built-in UV blockers. Buy it by the quart at home centers.

3   **4**   **5**

Mark for the sink cutout.

Draw the basin's dimensions on the bench top, using a framing square and a pencil.

Create the opening.

Cut along the pencil lines with a jigsaw. To reinforce the top, use stainless-steel screws to secure two of the cutout wood slats to the underside of the sink opening, one perpendicular to its boards on the right and one on the left.

Install the sink.

To keep from pinching your fingers, place a wood scrap on the bench top that you can shimmy out once the sink's in place. Then lift the sink and carefully ease the basin into the cutout in the bench top. Avoid back injury by doing this with a friend. Cast-iron sinks like this one can easily weigh 50 pounds or more.

Steps 6-9

81

Seal around the sink's edges.
Fill the gap between the bottom of the sink and the bench top with clear silicone caulk. For a crisp line, lay painter's tape along the sink lip and the wood top. Smooth with a soapy finger, then remove the tape.

Put on the upper shelf.
Secure it to the bench's sides and backsplash by driving 1½-inch screws into the predrilled holes.

Add curtain-rod hangers.
Twist eyebolts into the underside of the bench frame at the corners and in the center. Drill pilot holes first to make it easier to twist in the bolts.

SEE HOW IT'S DONE
View a step-by-step video for this outdoor bar sink project at **thisoldhouse.com/books**

Hang the curtains.
Cut three dowels
to the length of the
bench top's sides
and front to serve as
curtain rods. Slip the
dowels through the
eyebolts, then insert
through pole pockets
sewn along the tops
of the fabric curtains.
Crack open the
tequila, start mixing,
and toast to a job
well done.

What's their story?
KITCHEN SINKS

Long before the undermount sinks of today, the centerpiece
of early-20th-century kitchens was a freestanding single- or
double-bowl beauty propped up on shapely legs.

Perhaps because of dishwashers, or the sinks' behemoth
proportions, these leggy basins—and the built-in versions that
came after them—were ripped out of most kitchens.

Today you'll find them at salvage yards, where you can
choose not only the style you want, but the material, too.
Sinks from the 1860s were made by pouring ground glass
into molds that were then fired in kilns to form vitreous china.
Bulkier earthenware fireclay sinks with porcelain coatings also
debuted around this time. But it wasn't until the early 1900s,
when makers fused ground glass to hot metal, that porcelain-
coated cast-iron sinks became popular.

USE

A WOOD WINDOW

TO MAKE A

Picture Frame

Pained at the thought of this 1920s swing-out casement window ending up in a landfill, I plucked it from the trash outside a building on my New York City block and put it to good reuse as a wall-hung picture frame in my apartment. Similar windows sell for $25 to $50 at salvage yards. • The frame idea was inspired by a project sent to me by a *TOH* reader, who had mounted vintage family photos behind an old wood window's wavy glass panes. But rather than put my photos directly behind the glass, as she had done, I used $3 precut sage-green mats from the crafts store to add more depth. Unmatted, you get a slightly more modern look—the photos appear as if they were floating on the wall behind them. If that's the effect you're after, simply adhere the edges of the photos to the back side of the glass panes with clear archival mounting tape, and save yourself a few bucks on supplies. • Heck, if you live in a trash-picker's paradise like I do, start trolling the neighborhood now for an old window to convert, and this project will practically be free.

Supplies
WOOD WINDOW
LINT-FREE CLOTH
BEESWAX POLISH
WINDOW CLEANER
PENCIL
PHOTO MATS
2-INCH KRAFT PAPER
FRAMER'S TAPE
EYE HOOKS
PICTURE WIRE

Tools
RULER
PAPER CUTTER OR
UTILITY KNIFE
PLIERS

 2 HOURS $ ABOUT $30   SKILL LEVEL: <u>EASY</u>

HOW-TO

Start Here

Prep the window.
Use a lint-free cloth to rub beeswax polish on bare wood window sashes. (If you've got a painted sash, guard against lead by sealing the finish under a coat of polyurethane.) Spritz the glass with window cleaner.

Measure panes to determine mat sizes.
Jot down the length and width from the intersection points of the surrounding wood muntins, as mats will overlay the woodwork.

Trim the mats.
Slice off equal parts from the sides, top, and bottom so that the mats will be centered behind each pane. I used a paper cutter (shown), but a utility knife will also do the trick.

4   **5**   **6**   **7**

Tape photos to the mats.
Secure the photos to the backs of the mats with traditional flat-back kraft paper framer's tape or acid-free linen tape.

Arrange photos on the window.
Place each matted shot behind a window pane, and tape around its outer edges. Once all photos are in place, tape the inner edges to each other.

Check the placement.
You may have to move the photos ¼ inch or so and retape to ensure that each is centered behind its pane.

Add hanging hardware.
Screw in eye hooks on either side of the window frame. Thread picture wire through and twist the ends to secure. Then hang your frame on the wall and revel in your handiwork.

What's their story?
WOOD WINDOWS

The look and type of a home's windows say a lot about its architectural heritage. The number of panes or divided lights in a double-hung with two sashes that slide up and down, for instance, can help in discerning the difference between a 1730s Georgian-style house and a Greek Revival built 100 years later.

Designs of those early windows were driven by the availability of glass and the technology for making it. The majority was handmade in England and imported to America at great expense. The panes were often small.

By the late 1860s, domestic factories were turning out larger panes, allowing for more diversity in textures, patterns, and shapes, as well as affordable windows for Victorian-era homes and all new construction that followed.

USE AN

IRON WINDOW GUARD

TO MAKE A

Pot Rack

While some vintage iron guards were panels anchored within window surrounds, the vast majority were attached directly to a home's exterior wall framing with integrated straps. • The latter type is ideal for a pot rack because you can simply turn it on its side and use the existing fastener drill-outs in the straps to secure it to your wall. To suspend a rack from the ceiling, simply loop chain through these holes. • For this wall-mount rack, I bought a simple 3-foot-tall wrought-iron guard with two widely spaced twisted rails for $90. To hang the pots, I scoured the websites of online retailers in search of 10 wrought-iron S-hooks to match the rustic look of the rack. The 5-inch hooks I found were just $3 apiece, a mere dollar more than the industrial-looking steel ones you get at hardware stores. And like the salvaged window guard, the hooks were forged right here in the USA; each one bears the perfectly imperfect markings that give handcrafted wares so much character.

Supplies
WINDOW GUARD
S-HOOKS
WAX POLISH FOR METAL
LINT-FREE CLOTH
FASTENERS
BLACK SPRAY PAINT
ANCHORS

Tools
LEVEL
DRILL/DRIVER
DRILL BITS
RATCHET WRENCH

 1 HOUR $120  SKILL LEVEL: <u>EASY</u>

HOW-TO ➤

Start Here

Clean and
seal the iron.
Protect the iron
surface from
rust by rubbing
on wax polish
for metal. Buff
to a soft sheen.

Prep the
fasteners.
Spray shiny steel
bolts or screws
for hanging the
rack with black
spray paint so that
they'll match the
look of the iron.

Determine locations
for the fasteners.
Have a friend help hold the
rack against the wall where you
plan to install it; ideally there
will be studs to anchor into.
Use a level to check alignment,
and mark the center of the rack's
existing holes with a pencil.

4

5

6

Drill pilot holes.
Put a bit in your drill/
driver, and create a
path for the fasteners
that work best with
your wall type. For
drywall, I used 1½-inch-
long, ¼-inch lag
bolts and anchored
into the wall studs.

Secure the rack.
Steady the rack on
the wall and use
a ratchet wrench to
twist in the lag bolts.
Make installation
easier by screwing
all four bolts loosely
in place before going
back and tightening
each one.

Add the hooks.
Arrange them on
the top and bottom
rails. Now pull
your favorite pots
and pans from
those dark cabinet
recesses and hang
'em on your rack.

TIP

**Hang your
rack within
arm's reach
of the cooktop
so that pots
will be easily
accessible.**

What's their story?
IRON WINDOW GUARDS

A far cry from the prison-like bars sold today, 19th-century window guards actually enhanced the look of a home, making its inhabitants feel secure, not confined.

Used on windows in urban areas from Charleston to Chicago, they kept intruders out while letting air and light in. The strong wrought-iron bars were often embellished with decorative cast flowers, tassels, or medallions.

By the 1880s, dozens of companies competed to satisfy Victorian-era America's appetite for window guards and other ornamental ironwork. They hired skilled patternmakers, who followed all the latest European trends. Because of those guards' enduring style and sturdy construction, many still beautify streetscapes today.

USE

VICTORIAN-ERA TILES

TO MAKE A

Tabletop

Part of the fun of this project was rooting through the tile crates at a salvage shop with my friend Rosi. A mosaic maven who has covered her mailbox and even her home's foundation walls with stunning ceramic designs, Rosi has become my go-to for all things tile-related. In this case, I needed her help picking Victorian-era tiles for a top I wanted to make for an old wrought-iron table base. • Our first find was an 1890s 6-inch square depicting a Spanish Colonial mission with a graceful yellow archway and a brilliant blue sky, for $45. This, we agreed, would be the centerpiece. Next were four flowered accents, $8 each, and 30 marbled tiles from an old fireplace surround that we bought in bulk for $40. • Instead of dashing off once our shopping expedition was complete, Rosi offered to help arrange the tiles and mortar them in place. Like me, she was excited to see the forlorn table, which was missing its original glass top, transformed into something useful and beautiful.

Supplies

COLORFUL TILES
METAL TABLE BASE
MASONITE BOARD
POLYVINYL GLUE
TILE SPACERS
PENCIL
LATEX GLOVES
SAFETY GLASSES
MULTIPURPOSE CERAMIC-TILE ADHESIVE
SANDED GROUT
GROUT SEALER

Tools

JIGSAW
WET TILE SAW
GRINDSTONE OR TILE FILE
RUBBER SPATULA OR GROUT FLOAT
TILE GROUT SPONGE
TILE SQUEEGEE

 3+ HOURS   ABOUT $125   SKILL LEVEL: <u>MODERATE</u>

Start Here

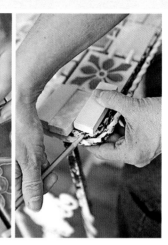

Lay out your tile design.

Use a jigsaw to cut a ⅛-inch-thick Masonite board to the inner dimensions of the tabletop's recess. Seal the porous material—front and back—with a coat of polyvinyl glue so that it won't absorb the tile adhesive. Set the board inside the base, and arrange the tiles on top.

Insert spacers.

Set ⅛- and ¼-inch plastic spacers (sizes will vary based on the layout) between the tiles to hold them in place.

Mark where to cut the tiles.

Use a pencil to draw cutlines on the tile bottoms where they overhang the edges of the tabletop's iron frame, being careful to follow the contours of the top.

4 **5** **6**

Cut tiles to size.
Wearing nonslip latex gloves and safety glasses, use a wet saw to slice the tiles along the pencil lines.

Smooth tile edges.
Use a grindstone (shown) or tile file to remove any jagged pieces.

Check the fit of the cut tiles.
Replace the tiles in the layout. If any still overhang the tabletop's iron frame, take off the excess with the grindstone.

➤➤

Steps 7-10

Don't forget...

Before you buy a vintage tile, check its back for stuck-on mortar, which is hard to remove without breaking the tile. If you find an encrusted tile that's just too good to pass up, try my trick: Gently chip off the mortar with a dental pick.

Adhere the tiles to the board.

Working from the center out, remove tiles one at a time, spread ceramic adhesive on their backs, and stick them on the board. Use a thick mastic, which allows you to build up a bed under thin tiles so that their surfaces are all level. Replace the spacers and let the adhesive set for 30 minutes, then remove them.

Set the tiles.

Position a flat board on top of the tiles, and weight it down. We used pattern weights from Rosi's costume shop (she makes clothes for theater and film), but a couple of bricks will do. Wait 24 hours for the adhesive to dry before removing the weights.

Grout the tiles.

Pop the board out of the table base. Use an old rubber spatula (shown) or a grout float to spread a thick coat of grout over the surface, then work it into the gaps. Sanded grout is best for filling gaps ⅛ inch wide or larger.

SEE HOW IT'S DONE
View a step-by-step video for this tiled tabletop project at thisoldhouse.com/books

10

Remove excess grout and insert the tabletop.
Remove the grout film from the tile faces with a tile squeegee. Spritz with water, and sponge off any remaining residue. Fit the tiled top back in the base, and let it set for 48 hours before applying a sealer to the grout lines. Then go ahead and use your stylish new table.

What's their story?

VICTORIAN-ERA TILES

Today, ceramic tiles are mostly unremarkable squares used to create washable surfaces in kitchens and baths. But a hundred years ago, tiles covered with vibrant colors, intricate patterns, and bold figures were also used to enliven the look of wainscot foyer walls and living room fireplace surrounds.

American tiles made from the late 1870s through the early 1900s were a practical and eye-catching feature in homes, as well as grand public buildings. They were the art of the everyday.

Inspired by European potteries that displayed their wares at the 1876 Centennial exhibition in Philadelphia, newly industrialized companies stateside began making their own tile designs. These Victorian-era examples feature embossed designs of flowers, shells, pastoral scenes, animals, and human figures. Each machine-pressed tile was a vision of uniformity thanks to smooth, purified clays, crisp details, and high-gloss glaze in colors ranging from dark amber to mint green with amethyst marbling.

USE

WOOD MOLDINGS

TO MAKE A

Window Box

A quarter doesn't buy much at salvage yards these days. Heck, it doesn't get you much anywhere. So imagine my surprise to find this ad in an online classifieds: "Antique salvaged wood molding for sale...twenty-five cents a foot. Bring a truck." *Better rent a U-Haul*, I thought. *That's a steal.* • Seriously, though, all I needed was 4 feet—enough to create a cottage-style window box to fill with cheery flowers. So off I went in my Honda hatchback, a crisp dollar bill in my pocket. • Among the piles of handsome moldings, I opted for a long length of window casing with a symmetrical, rather than tapered, profile on its face. This makes it easier to cut the angled corners when creating a rectangular planter box. And because I planned to nest a $7 plastic liner inside the box to hold the soil and flowers, I selected an extra-wide 8-inch casing that would fully conceal it. • This window box is a one-person project, but it's more fun with a helper. I enlisted my husband, Jon, to miter the corners of the box. Like great cut men who ready trim for the carpenter to install, he's got an eye for detail.

Supplies
8-INCH-WIDE MOLDING
½-INCH PRESSURE-
TREATED PLYWOOD
EXTERIOR WOOD GLUE
RUBBER GLOVES
1½-INCH SIDING NAILS
PENCIL
PLASTIC PLANTER
N100 DUST MASK
SAFETY GLASSES
SPAR URETHANE

Tools
CIRCULAR SAW
CLAMPS
HAMMER
DRILL/DRIVER
½-INCH PADDLE BIT
COMPOUND MITER SAW
NAILSET

 2 HOURS $ $18   SKILL LEVEL: <u>MODERATE</u>

Start Here

Build a
plywood box.
This is what you'll
mount the molding
on. Use a circular
saw to cut the
sides to a height
that's equal to the
molding width and
just slightly longer
than the plastic
planter that'll nest
inside. Glue and
clamp the sides,
and nail securely.

Add the box's bottom piece.
Cut a plywood board that's large enough to cover the side
panels' exposed edges. Attach the board with glue and nails.
Wait about 15 minutes for the adhesive to set. Then
flip the box right-side up, and insert the plastic planter.

Carpenter's golden rule
MEASURE TWICE, CUT ONCE.
BECAUSE WHEN THE SAW BLADE
SPINS, YOU ONLY GET ONE SHOT.

3

4

5

Add holes for drainage.
Mark the locations of the plastic planter's weep holes on the bottom of the plywood box. Remove the planter, and use a drill/driver fitted with a paddle bit to bore corresponding holes.

Make angled cuts.
Use a compound miter saw for 45 degree corners where the long front and two short-side molding strips meet. Cut just one miter on each of the three strips. You'll need to cut a second miter on the front strip, but only after you've determined its exact length and proper alignment on the plywood box.

Determine molding lengths.
Steady the mitered side strips against the plywood box, and mark for straight cuts where the rear end of the pieces will rest against the house. Hold the front strip against the box, and mark where to cut its second miter. Now make the last angled cut and two straight ones.

Steps 6-8

What's their story?
WOOD MOLDINGS

Used to soften the transitions between walls and adjacent windows, ceilings, floors, and doors, moldings' lineage dates to the ancient Greeks. Those early craftsmen created the profiles and the rules of proportion that we still use some 2,500 years later. Only the materials have changed. Rather than the original heavy stone, 18th-century American carpenters opted for more malleable, lighter-weight wood.

In those days, such ornamentation didn't come cheap: Each piece of crown, chair rail, casing, and baseboard was hand-planed. It wasn't until after the Civil War that manufacturers began mass-producing the trim, enabling builders to dress up even modest rooms from a catalog of affordable profiles.

Historically, molding profiles, which range from classical fluted designs to softly undulating S curves, echoed a home's architectural style.

6

Adhere the molding.
Apply exterior wood glue to the backs and mitered corners of the trim pieces, and adhere them to the front and sides of the plywood box. Use clamps to hold the molding in place while the glue cures.

7   8

**Secure
with nails.**
For extra strength,
tap in nails along
the top and bottom
edges of the
molding. Use a
nailset to recess
the heads.
Remove the clamps.

Insert the liner and fill with flowers.
Drop in the plastic planter, and add flowers; they'll boost
your home's curb appeal—and your outlook.

FINISHING TOUCH

*Most salvaged wood is covered in old
paint. Rather than remove the finish
with a wet stripper (dry stripping can release
lead dust), seal it under a clear top coat.*
SPAR URETHANE *in a spray can is a good
choice for outdoor projects like mine. That
patina is, after all, one of the things that give
vintage materials character.*

SALVAGE STAR

★ KARA O'BRIEN
ATLANTA, GA

/ SERIAL HOME REHABBER /

Look what one This Old House reader did!

"A RESTORED LIVING ROOM"

When *TOH* reader Kara O'Brien first stepped into the main living area of this 1920s fixer-upper, she saw a big, sun-filled space anchored by its original oak fireplace mantel. Sure, the plaster walls were cracked and the woodwork was caked in white paint, but for Kara, a contractor specializing in old-house renovations, that was nothing some Sheetrock and stripper couldn't fix. So Kara strapped on her tool belt and got busy.

1. MIRRORED MANTEL Kara hired a refinishing pro to take apart the mantel, dip its pieces in a chemical stripper, then power-wash, dry, and reassemble it. Once reinstalled, Kara sanded and finished it with an amber shellac like the one originally used to highlight the oak's eye-catching grain pattern. The restoration cost just $400, compared with about $3,000 to have a similar mantel custom made from new wood.

2. POCKET DOORS A pair of stained-glass pocket doors, which slide on a track into recesses within the walls, came from a local salvage shop that was going out of business. Lucky find! Kara paid $500 for the doors, sold "as is" with layers of old paint clinging to the white pine stiles and rails. She stripped and refinished them herself, patching old hardware holes with scrap wood.

3. BRASS CHANDELIER The living room was missing its original ceiling fixture, so Kara set off in search of a vintage replacement. She settled on a four-light brass chandelier from a salvage dealer, for $400. It had been rewired, polished, buffed, and coated with clear lacquer to prevent tarnishing. The only catch was, the chandelier didn't have its original shades. Kara found the milky white reproductions at a home center for just $6 each.

USE

A STAINED-GLASS WINDOW

TO MAKE A

Wall Cabinet

The graphic diamond pattern on this red-and-amber-colored stained-glass sidelight really complemented the more Mod furnishings in my apartment. But the window's tall, narrow proportions are what made it ideal for the door of a wall-mount cabinet I wanted to create for an awkward recess in my dining room. I needed a place to store wine glasses and champagne flutes that was outside the mayhem of my kitchen. • The other great thing about the window: It was free! A friend had it gathering dust against a wall in his garage, and he was nice enough to give it to me during one of his spring-cleaning purges. Windows like these start about $200 at salvage yards, but I've seen them for half as much at antiques fairs and through online classifieds. • The only other major expenses were about $24 for the preprimed pine to build the cabinet, $20 for the birch plywood back, and $10 for an old bin pull to use as a door handle. You're going to roll your eyes at me, but I actually got my pull for free, too. I took it off a built-in cabinet one of my neighbors had trashed. I always carry a little multitool in my bag, because you never knew when you might need a screwdriver.

Supplies
STAINED-GLASS SIDELIGHT
BIN PULL
PREPRIMED 1× PINE
½-INCH BIRCH PLYWOOD
PENCIL
WOOD GLUE
1½-INCH TRIM-HEAD SCREWS
HINGES
GLOSS LATEX PAINT
SANDPAPER

Tools
TAPE MEASURE
CIRCULAR SAW
FRAMING SQUARE
CLAMPS
DRILL/DRIVER
CHISEL
PAINTBRUSH
SCREWDRIVER

 4 HOURS $ ABOUT $250   SKILL LEVEL: <u>DIFFICULT</u>

HOW-TO ⟫

Start Here

Create the cabinet parts.
Cut the 1× pine sides to the height of the window, using a circular saw or table saw. The top, bottom, and shelves should be 1½ inches smaller than the window's width. Using a pencil and a framing square, mark on the sides where the shelves will go.

Assemble the pieces.
Use wood glue to adhere the top and bottom panels between the side walls. Secure the assembly with clamps, then slip the shelves into place, using the pencil marks as guides. The back panel goes on later.

TIP ☞ To clean hard-to-reach crevices on stained-glass windows, I just dip a Q-tip in denatured alcohol and gently wipe away dust and dirt.

3 **4** **5**

**Secure the
assembly with
screws.**
Use your drill/driver
to drive 1½-inch
trim-head screws
through the side
walls and into the
ends of the top and
bottom panels
and the shelves.

**Create hinge
mortises in the
cabinet front.**
Mark for the
hinges about
4 inches from the
top and bottom of
the cabinet. Scoop
out the wood to the
thickness of the
hinge with a chisel,
its beveled edge
pointing down.
Flip the chisel's
bevel to shave
the surface.

Determine hinge placement on the door.
Put the closed hinges in the cabinet mortises, and place the
stained-glass door squarely on top to mark where the hinges
line up on its wood frame. Create the mortises for the hinges
on the door's inside face.

Steps 6-9

6

7

8

Add the
back panel.
Cut a sheet of
½-inch plywood
to the dimensions
of your cabinet,
and secure it with
trim-head screws.

Paint the
cabinet.
Brush the cabinet
with two coats
of gloss latex paint,
sanding between
coats. Let sit for
a few hours to dry.
Leave the inside
of the back panel
unfinished to add
contrast and depth,
as I did here, or
paint it to match
the cabinet.

Secure the door
to the cabinet.
Drill pilot holes
for the hinge
screws, place the
cabinet on its side
next to the glass
door, and attach
the hardware.

9

Add the handle and hang your cabinet. Stand the cabinet up and mark for the bin pull's fasteners. Bore pilot holes and drive in the screws. Next, hang your cabinet, being sure to anchor into a wall stud. This will ensure that your stained-glass door and any breakables inside remain safe. Now pull out a flute and pour yourself some celebratory champagne.

What's their story?

STAINED-GLASS WINDOWS

Unlike their Christian-themed predecessors, which told biblical stories through pictures, the colorful architectural stained-glass windows in Craftsman, Queen Anne, and Tudor houses were used for their beauty and function. Installed as sidelights flanking a front door, as transoms above standard double-hung or casement windows, or even in place of an operable window in a dining area, stair hall, or bathroom, stained glass provides privacy and can obscure a view without blocking natural light.

Many residential stained-glass designs were inspired by masterworks from artists such as Louis Comfort Tiffany, whose depictions of autumn landscapes and cascading wisteria vines are still copied today. Arts and Crafts–style oak trees and cherry blossoms by the California architectural firm Greene & Greene and stylized chevron patterns popularized in the early 1900s by Frank Lloyd Wright have also been widely imitated.

USE

WOOD CORBELS

TO MAKE A

Bedside Table

I've got one of those old-timey iron beds. You know, the kind that's so high you have to take a running leap to get into it. So instead of scouring antiques stores for an equally tall bedside table, I built one myself. • For the table base, I anchored a pair of salvaged corbels to the wall. The top is an oxblood-colored slate roof shingle rescued from a demolished church; it has two little holes where it used to be fastened to the roof sheathing. I bought all the parts at a New Jersey salvage yard for $70. The result: a rustic-looking built-in that's just the right height and doesn't take up an inch of floor space. • Rarely used on houses built after the 1940s, most carved wood corbels seen today are still attached to older buildings or scattered around architectural salvage yards. My matched set had once decorated the porch of a late-19th-century rowhouse in Philadelphia. Far too weather-beaten to reuse outdoors, the corbels were perfect for my indoor project.

Supplies
2 WOOD CORBELS
LARGE ROOF SLATE
PENCIL
3½-INCH DECK SCREWS
VELCRO TAPE
MINERAL OIL
LINT-FREE CLOTH

Tools
2-FOOT LEVEL
DRILL/DRIVER
⅛-INCH DRILL BIT
⁵⁄₁₆-INCH PADDLE BIT
FILE

 1 HOUR $70   SKILL LEVEL: <u>EASY</u>

Start Here

Determine where to hang the corbels.
Center one corbel on a stud at the desired height, and use a pencil to trace a horizontal line on the wall across its top. Have a friend hold the corbel in place while you use a 2-foot level to lay out the position of the second corbel.

Create paths for the fasteners.
Steady the corbels on the lines, and bore two ⅛-inch pilot holes through their tops at a 45-degree angle. Use a 5⁄16-inch paddle bit to drill recesses in which to sink the screwheads.

TIP
To find wall studs, I hammer tiny holes along the top of baseboards with a finishing nail until I hit wood. Then I simply cover the holes with caulk.

4

5

6

Install the corbels.
Use 3½-inch deck screws to attach the corbels to the wall, anchoring them to the studs. Once secured at their tops, bore a straight pilot hole in each corbel's bottom section and drive in a third screw for extra support.

Add the roof slate top.
Rather than risk breaking the slate by drilling holes for fasteners, hold it in place with double-sided Velcro tape stuck on the corbel tops. Smooth any jagged edges with a file.

Condition the slate.
Apply a coat of mineral oil with a lint-free cloth to remove scratches and brighten the stone's natural color.

What's their story?
WOOD CORBELS

Wood corbels, which were often positioned at a 90-degree angle between a porch's posts and its ceiling or tucked under roof eaves, were integral to the "gingerbread" millwork decorating Victorian-era facades.

In the 1890s, ornate corbels were mass-produced for use on Queen Anne houses. Ordered through catalogs and transported on expanding railway lines, they came in a wide variety of wood types, in sizes 4 inches to 3 feet tall. Designs ranged from solid serpentine and quarter-round forms to more decorative shapes with applied droplet details and side panels pierced with intricate scrollwork.

USE

A CAST-IRON URN

TO MAKE A

Garden Fountain

Age and whether an urn is stamped by its manufacturer are major factors in determining its value. This one has no maker's mark. And because it has very little rust and no traces of old paint, I'd wager that it isn't more than 15 or 20 years old. Though far from an antique, it's handsome, and at $150 the price was right. • Victorian-era urns from the late 1800s, when the vessels first came into vogue as garden decor, can cost $750 or much more, especially for a 3-footer like this one. But as lovely as those originals are, they aren't ideal for creative reuse projects. Case in point: I not only planned to give this urn to my *TOH* coworker Alex, but also to fill it full of rust-inducing water instead of flowers. • The only other major expense for this fountain project was the submersible recirculating bubbler, which I got at a home center for $25. The rest was sweat equity. And to be honest, Alex and I pulled it all together so easily and on such a nice, breezy day that we barely had to wipe our brows.

Supplies
CAST-IRON URN
FOUNTAIN PUMP
2 RUBBER STOPPERS
SILICONE CAULK
CLEAR SPRAY SEALER

Tools
UTILITY KNIFE
CAULK GUN
GARDEN HOSE

🕐 1 HOUR 💲 ABOUT $175 ➤ SKILL LEVEL: <u>EASY</u>

Start Here

Prep the pump
cord and rubber
stoppers.
Use a utility knife to
slit and cut a center
hole in two rubber
stoppers; slip the
pump cord through.
I used a white sink-
drain plug, then a
black toilet flush-
valve seal to cover
it. Get them at the
hardware store for
about $2 each.

Thread the
cord through
the urn.
Fit the electrical
plug in the
drainage hole in
the bottom of the
urn, and thread
the cord through.

Secure the
stoppers.
Squeeze silicone
caulk around the
edges of the drain
plug, and insert it
in the hole. Place
the valve seal on
top of the plug; to
create a watertight
seal, caulk around
its edges and where
it wraps around
the cord.

 SEE HOW IT'S DONE
View a step-by-step video for
this garden fountain project at
thisoldhouse.com/books

4

5

What's their story?
CAST-IRON URNS

In Victorian times, having iron in your garden was a status symbol. Not just any chunk of ore, but an ornate cast-iron urn.

In the second half of the 19th century, a garden with vine-filled urns signified wealth and culture. The trend was led by America's emerging middle class, which could devote land to flowers and winding paths rather than farm crops.

Cast-iron urns from the 1850s were modeled after ancient Greek and Roman architecture, with fluted sides, scalloped cornices around the rims, and boxy pedestal bases. Handles sometimes took the form of snakes or mythological beasts.

By 1880, urns were more fanciful, with the sorts of rococo embellishments— cherubs, shells, and flowers— that characterized flamboyant 18th-century French furniture.

Fit in the pump; protect the urn's finish.
To raise or level the pump in the bottom of the urn, wedge smooth rocks underneath it. To retain the urn's existing finish, spray with a rust-inhibiting sealer before filling with water or exposing to the elements.

Finish by filling with water.
Position the urn where it will be a focal point in your garden, then use a garden hose to fill with water. Plug the pump into a GFCI outdoor outlet, and relax as your new fountain gurgles away.

USE

A WOOD INTERIOR DOOR

TO MAKE A

Headboard

As much as you might be smitten with a certain distressed finish or warm wood patina, panel configuration is the first thing to consider when shopping for a door to transform into a headboard. Be sure to pick one with evenly spaced squares or rectangles that are the same size and shape. That way, when you turn the door on its side, the design will be symmetrical. Craftsman-style five-panel doors with rectangles stacked one on top of the other like ladder rungs are ideal, as are Art Deco–style doors with a single recessed panel in the center. I chose a ladder-type door in oak, which typically ranges in price from $65 to $200 at salvage yards. • Door height is also key; most are between 70 and 96 inches. While you might be lucky enough to find a match for a standard 76-inch-wide king-size bed, for anything smaller, you'll have to cut one down. For my 60-inch queen bed, I trimmed from the top and bottom to maintain the door's proportions. • Completing my wall-hung headboard are a pair of sconces I mounted on either end of the door. They make great reading lamps but also create a nice mood-setting glow in the bedroom.

 1 DAY $375 SKILL LEVEL: DIFFICULT

1 **2** **3**

Start Here

Measure your door.
Consider mattress widths to determine how much you'll need to trim off of the door. A twin is 39 inches wide, a full is 54, a queen is 60, and a king is 76. Allow a few more inches if you want to add sconces, as I did. Use a combination square to mark the cutlines.

Trim it to size.
Use a circular saw to cut your door. To create a guide for the saw to follow, place a steel ruler alongside your cutlines and clamp it to the door.

Patch holes.
Fill the void in the edge of the door where the lock used to be by tapping in a wood scrap. To fill surface holes, make a putty out of sawdust and clear-drying white craft glue. Blend until it's the consistency of creamy peanut butter, and spread with a putty knife.

4

5

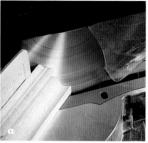

Create the crown for the top.
Mark the length of the door's face on a strip of solid crown molding. Cut to size, mitering ends at 45-degree angles (a). Use the offcuts to create decorative returns for the door's outside edges, giving the top a finished look (b).

Steps 6-8

Sand the surface.
For stripped doors, remove splinters and round over rough edges with a random-orbit sander that's hooked up to a wet-dry vac to limit dust. For painted ones, first remove the old finish with an eco-safe gel stripper; dry stripping can release lead dust into the air.

TIP ☞ To hang heavy stuff like this headboard, I like to use a French cleat. Here's how to make one:

1. Have the lumberyard run a length of ¾-inch plywood through a table saw with the blade at 45 degrees, creating a beveled lip on one edge. 2. Cut the strip in two, and screw one section to your wall studs with its lip facing up and away from the wall. 3. Secure the other strip to the headboard with the lip facing down and away. 4. Lift the headboard into place so that its beveled strip interlocks with the opposing one on the wall.

6   7

BRAD NAILERS make installing molding as easy as pulling a trigger. Better still are new, cordless ones. Mine, shown at right, relies on a battery and fuel cell to sink 18-gauge nails called brads. Traditional nail guns are powered by an unwieldy plug-in air compressor and are tethered to a hose.

Secure the crown.
Squeeze a bead of glue on the crown's back and press into place. Reinforce the bond by tapping in finishing nails about every 6 inches. I used a brad nailer to speed the process.

Seal the wood.
To restore the door's luster and highlight the grain pattern, use a lint-free cloth to apply a natural beeswax polish. Then buff it with a lint-free cloth to impart a soft sheen. Recoat and buff periodically to keep up the finish.

Install the sconces.

Mark where you want the fixtures to be. Fit a drill/ driver with a paddle bit, and bore holes through which to fish wires. Secure the sconce back- plates to the door using the screws provided, and hook up the lights. Now hang your new headboard, fluff up your pillows, and take a well- deserved break.

What's their story?
WOOD INTERIOR DOORS

One way to tell a new house from an old one is by its interior doors. Open one and give it a good knuckle-rapping.

Doors in homes built before 1950 are typically made of solid wood, whether oak, maple, chestnut, or mahogany. They've got heft, and they make a satisfying thump when you knock. They also have sturdy stiles and rails that frame panels in a variety of configurations, depending on the home's architectural style.

Compare that with new, hollow doors—made of veneered plywood or fiberboard—which tend to be lightweight and echoey, and have about as much detail as an ironing board.

This isn't to say that all houses built in the past 60 years have hollow doors. Some newer homes do have the good stuff. It's just that solid-wood doors in anything other than paint-grade pine can be hard to come by. Aside from going to a mill shop, salvage yards are pretty much your only source.

USE

WOOD INTERIOR SHUTTERS

TO MAKE

Cabinet Doors

Even with the advent of display-worthy flat-screen TVs, there are still the wires, cable box, DVD player, and audio equipment to contend with. I'm of the camp that believes it's better to keep it all under wraps. So is my *TOH* coworker Alexandra. • After building her own media-storage shelves, Alex simply got tired of looking at all that equipment when it wasn't in use. Rather than make a custom door or pay big bucks to have a mill shop build one for her, she bought two raised-panel mahogany shutters at a salvage yard for $75. Hinged together like a bifold closet door, they neatly hide the equipment. And painted the same glossy white as the shelves, the disparate parts blend together perfectly. • Another bonus of integrating vintage finds into her upgrade project? Well, that'd be getting me to come over and pitch in with the labor. Alex knew I wouldn't be able to resist. Clever girl.

 3 HOURS   ABOUT $90   SKILL LEVEL: <u>MODERATE</u>

HOW-TO ➡➡

Start Here

Fill old notches.
Use epoxy wood filler to patch the mortised edges where the old hinge hardware used to be. Let dry, and use a rasp (shown) or sandpaper to smooth the buildup. To turn two single shutters into a bifold, you must also remove the rabbets (light-blocking strips where opposing pairs of shutters come together). Cut these off with a jigsaw to create smooth edges.

Cut new shutter mortises.
Steady the swinging leaf of the wraparound hinges on the shutter edge that'll attach to the cabinet, 3 inches from its top and bottom. Score around the hinges with a utility knife; chisel out wood so hinges fit flush.

Paint both shutters.
Brush on primer, let dry, and sand. Then top with two coats of gloss latex paint, sanding between coats. Once dry, drill pilot holes and secure the shutter hinges with the screws provided.

Cut mortises in the cabinet.
Steady the hinged shutter in the opening, and use a pencil to trace around the L-shaped portion on the hinges where they'll attach to the cabinet. Score along the outline and chisel out the mortises.

Create the bifold.
Stand both shutters back-to-back, edges up. At 6 inches from their tops and bottoms, place the no-mortise hinges so that the barrel is between the two shutters. Drill pilot holes, and drive in the hinge screws.

Attach the shutters.
Fit the shutter hinges in the shelving unit's mortises, drill pilot holes, and drive in the screws.

Add a door pull.
Drill a hole for the post that's centered on the leading door. Insert the post from the back, and twist on the pull. Now open your new cabinet door, flip on the tube, and veg out.

What's their story?

WOOD INTERIOR SHUTTERS

Interior shutters were the original window treatments, used for centuries to create privacy, control natural light, and add architectural detail to rooms.

In the 18th and 19th centuries, Federal-style and Greek Revival houses in the North typically had solid-panel shutters, which, in addition to blocking unwanted views and sunlight, helped insulate windows against the cold.

In the South, interior shutters had movable louvers surrounded by a stile-and-rail frame. With the center louvers open, homeowners could let cool breezes into the house while still partially deflecting the hot sun.

SEE HOW IT'S DONE
View a step-by-step video for this shutter door project at **thisoldhouse.com/books**

USE

CERAMIC BATH ACCESSORIES

TO MAKE A

Jewelry Holder

If they can cradle tumblers and toothpaste, then vintage ceramic bathroom accessories can just as easily corral my husband's cuff links and my necklaces. Such was the thinking behind this his-and-hers holder. • Most ceramic accessories have unglazed backs and edges where they were adhered to a wall and surrounded by tiles. Some, like the tumbler and toothbrush holders I got for $30 each at a salvage yard, have glazed edges and predrilled screw holes so that they could be surface-mounted. This makes them easier to reuse in rooms other than tiled baths because you can simply screw the holders directly to the wall or to a wood mounting board, as I did here. • For a decorative touch, I covered the front of the mounting board—a curvy basswood plaque I got for $8 at a crafts store—with a scrap of wallpaper, giving it a more luxe look than a simple coat of paint would. If you don't have any leftover wallpaper kicking around your house, you can usually find a foot or so for a couple of bucks, or even free, in the sample bins at home-decorating supply shops. If you plan to share the holder with a significant other, be sure to pick a pattern that's universally appealing. You both gotta like it to use it.

Supplies
SANDPAPER
CERAMIC TUMBLER AND
TOOTHBRUSH HOLDER
WOOD PLAQUE
SEMIGLOSS LATEX PAINT
WALLPAPER
WALLPAPER PASTE
PENCIL
DECORATIVE SCREWS

Tools
PAINTBRUSH
PLASTIC SMOOTHER
UTILITY KNIFE
RULER
SCREWDRIVER

 1 HOUR   ABOUT $70   SKILL LEVEL: <u>EASY</u>

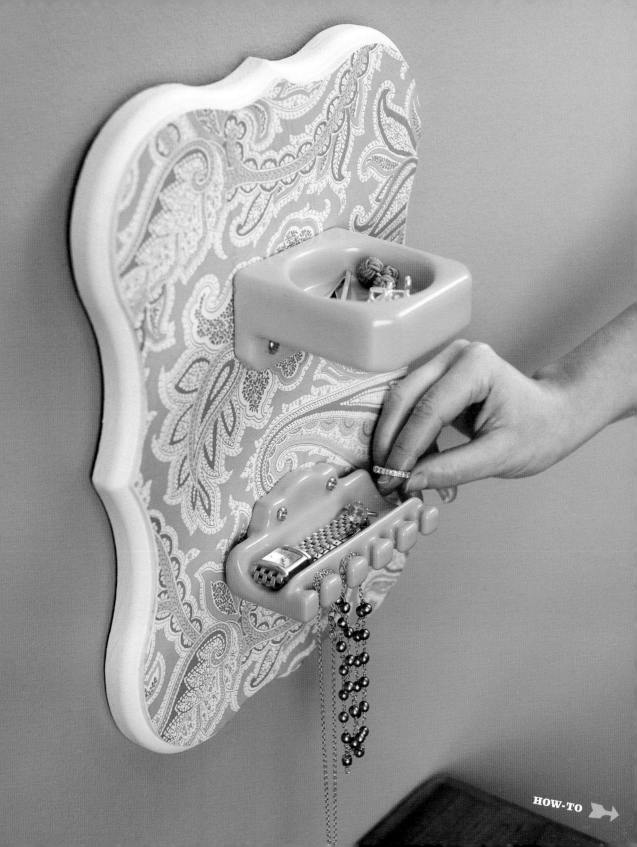

HOW-TO ➡

Start Here

1

Paint the plaque's edges.
First sand the surface smooth, then brush on a coat of semigloss latex.

2

Apply the wallpaper paste.
Weigh down the corners of the paper to keep it from curling, and brush on a generous layer of paste. I prefer a premixed, eco-friendly clay-based paste for most jobs.

3

Adhere the paper to the plaque.
Press it down with your hands. Go over the surface with a plastic wallpaper smoother to work out air bubbles.

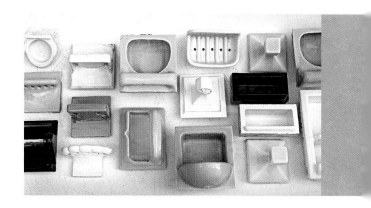

4 **5** **6**

Trim the paper to fit.
Flip the plaque facedown, and trace along its edge with a utility knife to remove excess wallpaper.

Mark where the holders will go.
Center them on the plaque, leaving enough room in between to set items down easily on the lower holder. Use a ruler and pencil to mark for the fasteners.

Secure the holders to the plaque.
Position them on the marks, and fasten in place using decorative screws. Use this designated landing spot for all things bling, to tidy up the dresser top.

FINISHING TOUCH

Instead of buying a quart of paint for a small job like this, I get **COLOR SAMPLES.** *Paint companies sell 2-ounce pots for as little as $5 each.*

What's their story?
CERAMIC BATH ACCESSORIES

All house parts have their day. For ceramic bath accessories, it was an era: 1930s Art Deco. That's when toothbrush holders were shaped like seashells, and recessed toilet-paper holders with stepped edges stylishly dispensed tissue. Unlike their all-white predecessors, these came in a rainbow of colors, from canary yellow to dusky blue.

Thanks to an ample supply of reclaimed bathroom materials at salvage yards today, it's easy to find period accessories. Just keep in mind that tile-in versions often have old mortar stuck to their backs, which you'll have to gently scrape off. Screw-in versions typically come ready to install.

Dressing Up Your Home With Salvage

➡ TIPS FOR INSTALLING VINTAGE HOUSE PARTS TO GIVE YOUR ROOMS A STYLE BOOST

Not everything has to be creatively repurposed. Reusing rescued elements, such as a carved-wood newel post to punctuate the end of a staircase, is a great way to amp up the vintage character of an old house or add a lived-in look to a new one. But finding the perfect piece can be tricky. I say this having once bought an Art Deco–era pedestal sink that was too wide for my powder room. So just as I now carry my measurements whenever I shop, you too can learn from my mistakes and, even better, my successes in sorting the treasures from the trash.

Interior woodwork ➤

The bulk of what you'll find at salvage yards is made from wood: carved mantels, paneled doors, double-hung windows, stair spindles, and shutters. Condition and price vary widely. Some dealers sell only near-mint or restored pieces ready for installation; others sell dusty, paint-caked items to DIYers willing to put in a little sweat equity in order to pay less. Cleaning, fitting, and repairing old wood elements can be a lot of work, but the rewards of preserving a finely crafted piece that's been around for years, and enjoying something that's unique to your home, can far outweigh the effort.

DOORS

How to shop
- Bring doorway measurements: from the inside of one side jamb to the other, and from the threshold to head jamb. Measure in several places, and take the largest numbers. Note the direction of the door swing and which side the hinges are on.
- Look for a door that's ¼ inch narrower and shorter than the opening to provide extra clearance, or one that can be cut down to size.
- Choose stained or stripped doors when possible, to avoid having to deal with lead paint.

What to avoid
- Twisted, cupped, or warped wood.
- Loose stiles and rails that surround center panels.
- Cracks or gashes in the wood, unless you plan to paint over repairs.
- Lockset holes that don't match the location or type of latch on the jamb. You don't want to buy a door drilled for a box-shaped mortise lock to install in a jamb that's bored for a round, tubular-type lock.

Expect to pay $60 to $250 per door.

WINDOWS

How to shop
- Bring dimensions. For a pre-hung window, measure the rough opening between the studs and from the sill to window header. Get a unit that's 2 inches smaller so that you can shim it to fit. For replacement sashes in a double-hung window, measure the height of the existing sashes and

Stained glass hung from eyebolts brightens the view.

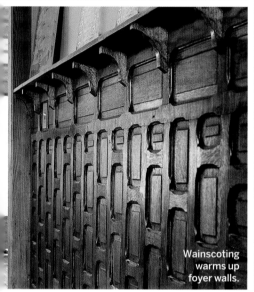

Wainscoting warms up foyer walls.

A shapely newel post turns stairs into a focal point.

the space between the side jams. Check the dimensions in three places and note the smallest.

• Get a window that requires the least amount of repair to its wood muntins and corner joints.

• Consider stained-glass windows as accents to use above doorways or in place of a double-hung sash.

What to avoid

• Incomplete units. It's hard to find an exact match for a missing sash. Trim, weights, pulleys, and sash cords are replaceable.

• Mismatched glass. A modern glass replacement pane will stick out like a sore thumb when surrounded by original wavy-glass panes.

• Damaged leading in stained glass. The metal that surrounds glass pieces can become stressed or cracked, causing windows to bulge, glass to rattle, and joints to loosen.

Expect to pay $40 to $150 for a double-hung, and $100 to $1,500 or more for a stained-glass window.

TRIM AND STAIR PARTS

How to shop

• Look for stained pieces that don't need to be stripped. If you love the look of old chipped paint, be sure to seal the surface under a clear coat to keep any lead contained.

• Don't expect to find enough moldings to finish an entire room. Salvaged trim is best for replacing a single door or window casing with something **CONTINUED ON NEXT PAGE** more dramatic. For larger amounts, take a salvaged profile to a millshop for duplicating.

• For paneled wainscoting, ask for a blueprint or a detailed drawing of how it was originally installed on the wall, to aid with reassembly. Even a photo taken before it was dismantled can help you visualize how it will fit in your space.

• Look for a newel post that matches your stair configuration. Ones with plinth-block bases stand flush with the floor. Newels with notched bases follow the rise of a step. For either type, make sure the newel's top works with your rail connection.

What to avoid

• Dry rot and excessive wormholes.

• Aggressively refinished profiles—fine details can be sanded off.

• Short stair spindles for new balustrades, unless you plan to build up the framing or add plinths under each spindle. Standard handrail height is 34 to 38 inches, so spindles beneath should be at least 31 inches.

Expect to pay 25 cents to $10 per linear foot for moldings, depending on the profile and width. Paneled wainscoting is $250 to $400 per 3-by-6-foot section. Beadboard runs about $5 per square foot. Newels range from $100 to $1,500, depending on size and decoration. Spindles can be had for $7 apiece.

FIREPLACE MANTELS

How to shop

• Bring dimensions of the firebox opening, the tile or stone border

A vintage wood mantel adds instant patina to a new fireplace.

that surrounds it, and the wall on which the mantel will be anchored.

• Stick to wood mantels with a large opening in the center, or noncombustible stone mantels. Modern fire code requires at least 6 inches of clearance from the firebox at both the top and sides.

• Look for a mantel that matches the style and era of your house, or one that incorporates existing molding profiles in the room.

What to avoid

• Exceptionally ornate mantels. Unless you live in a Queen Anne mansion, these can overpower the room.

• Undersize mantels. You may be able to bump up the height with blocks under the legs and extend the center with panels, but you'll need to have a shelf made for the top.

Expect to pay $450 to $2,500 for a wood mantel, depending on type, condition, size, detailing, and whether it has a mirrored top called an overmantel. Stone mantels, typically made of slate, marble, or limestone, start at about $1,750.

Plumbing fixtures ⟩⟩

Salvage yards are famous for stockpiling vintage sinks, cast-iron tubs, and freestanding fin-style radiators. Plumbing and heating fixtures are often sold "as is." So before you buy, keep in mind that the tub you covet may need to be repaired, refinished, or—most difficult—retrofitted to comply with modern plumbing codes. You don't want to end up with a 5-foot-long planter in the backyard when you're counting on a period soaker for the master bath.

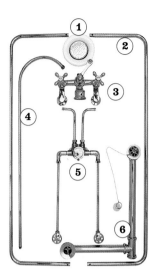

TUBS

How to shop

• Bring your bathroom dimensions, including those for a tub recess, and note where the drain is located.

• Climb in, lie back, and see how it feels. You can't beat an old claw-foot tub for comfort. They're perfectly angled for reclining, and they hold more water than a modern tub of the same length because the overflow drains are higher (typically 16 to 18 inches above the tub floor compared with 12 to 14 inches today).

What to avoid

• Rust spots, dents, and missing feet, which are particularly hard to match.

• Worn and stained glaze on the inside. Unlike peeling paint on the outside, which you can strip and refinish yourself, interior porcelain reglazing is a job best left to the pros.

• Tubs with an undersize or nonexistent overflow. **CONTINUED ON NEXT PAGE**

HOW TO PLUMB A CLAW-FOOT FOR A SHOWER

Reminiscent of ancient Roman soakers, claw-foot tubs have an elegant look. But plumbing one for a shower can be a challenge because you can't hide water lines behind the wall. This Victorian-style reproduction setup with exposed fittings (available from specialty bath suppliers) solves the problem by tapping into pipes that extend through the floor.

1. Showerhead
2. Wraparound curtain rod, which suspends from ceiling
3. Faucet with diverter to toggle between tub and shower
4. Shower riser that extends from faucet and attaches to showerhead
5. Pressure-balance valve to prevent scalding; attached to water supply lines with shutoffs
6. Drain and waste water overflow system

A claw-foot tub is a sculptural addition in a simple bathroom.

That's a flooded bathroom waiting to happen, and a violation of most local plumbing codes. The overflow should be at least 2½ inches in diameter.

Expect to pay $150 to $750 in "as is" condition. Reglazing a porcelain tub interior starts at $250.

BATHROOM SINKS

How to shop
• Keep in mind the style of your bathroom. Highly decorated baths can accommodate a curvy or elaborate sink, but contemporary ones call for clean lines.
• Consider space and installation constraints. Wall-mount sinks typically take up less room than pedestal sinks, but they are heavy and require support in the wall framing.
• Factor in the material. Porcelain-coated fireclay, a type of earthenware, and vitreous china sinks tend to be finer than enameled cast-iron ones and typically don't require refinishing. But they can also be heavy.

What to avoid
• Bad crazing (crackling finish) on porcelain. This can't be remedied. But a little crazing gives the sink a beautiful patina. Just make sure the surface is smooth to the touch.
• Rust spots, dents, chips, and deep scratches in cast-iron sinks. Like tubs, they will probably need to be refinished. Reglazing can add $100 or more to the price.

Expect to pay $600 to $1,200 for fireclay or vitreous china, and about $150 for a cast-iron sink, not including reglazing.

A marble-topped console sink has a furniture-like look.

FAUCETS AND FITTINGS

How to shop
• Factor in the faucet type. Choices include single handles, ones that bridge hot and cold connections, and wall-mount faucets.
• Measure the distance between the centers of your sink's faucet holes and make sure the fittings match the span. Openings are typically 4, 6, or 8 inches apart.

What to avoid
• Incomplete sets. Missing faucet parts are almost impossible to find.
• Badly pitted chrome finishes. You can pay to have old fittings replated, but this is a labor of love, not logic.

Expect to pay $175 to $400 for a fully restored faucet set with handles.

CAST-IRON RADIATORS

How to shop
• Figure out which type you need. Radiators with just one intake pipe at the bottom can only be used with steam systems. Forced-hot-water radiators have two pipes—one for intake and a second that recycles cooled water back to the furnace—and the sections need to be connected at the top. Some steam systems can also use two-pipe radiators.
• Try to match replacements with others in your house. Most yards stock tall, ornate Victorian-era radiators as well as squat, utilitarian designs from the 1940s.
• Replace leaky or broken radiators with ones equal in size and output.

What to avoid
• Throwing good money after bad. Stick to yards that test their stock for leaks and handle the dirty job of sandblasting units to remove old paint. Avoid unrestored radiators—they may leak or function as poorly as the ones being replaced.

Expect to pay $10 to $30 per fin-shape section for radiators tested for leaks, slightly more for ones that have been refinished.

Hardware ⇒→

In the far corners and back rooms of many salvage yards reside bins of old door hardware. Here's where you'll find that missing cast-bronze knob to restore a period entryway, or a pair of old iron strap hinges to lend provenance to a reproduction cabinet.

DOORKNOBS

How to shop

• When looking for a single replacement knob, bring its mate. You don't want to rifle through boxes of hardware only to discover that the knob you got doesn't fit on the spindle.
• Bring the measurement of your door's thickness and compare it with the span between the knobs, to ensure a snug fit.
• Choose complete knob sets, including the rosette, spindle, and the set screw that attaches it to the knob.

What to avoid

• Extreme wear, such as deep scratches and chips in glass knobs and pits and dents in metal ones.
• Locksets on doors that need to be latched and secured, because most don't have the original key. You can, however, use a pair of old knobs with a new dead bolt.
• Glass or brass knobs that have come loose **CONTINUED ON NEXT PAGE**

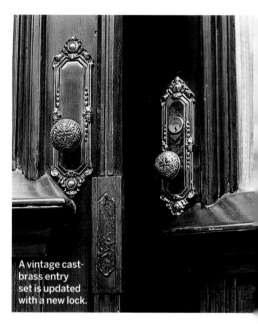

A vintage cast-brass entry set is updated with a new lock.

KNOW YOUR KNOB PARTS

Old doorknobs and locks have many working parts, some of which can be hard to replace. To be sure you get a complete set, check for the following:

1. Shank The metal collar that wraps a knob's base and contains the socket to receive the spindle. Make sure it fits tightly.
2. Mortise lock The box-shape locking mechanism that was standard in doors made before 1940. The spindle fits through a square hole in the lock, and when turned it triggers the latch. Old knob sets, however, will still work in the same way with the tubular bored locks made today.
3. Spindle The threaded rod that links a pair of knobs and fits through the lockset to control the latch.
4. Rosette A metal disk that fits around the shank, covering the hole in the door. A backplate that also covers the keyhole—called an escutcheon—can be used instead.
5. Setscrew The small screw in the shank that fixes the knob to the spindle. Make sure that its slotted head hasn't been stripped.

from their shanks, or collars—this can't be fixed.

Expect to pay $25 and up for a pair of simple white-porcelain knobs, and about $35 for clear faceted-glass ones. Ornamental cast-brass or cast-bronze knobs are $50 and $250 per pair.

HINGES

How to shop
• Consider the age and style of your house, and choose hinges that echo the design or finish of other decorative details in the room, such as wall sconces or the kitchen faucet.
• Keep utility in mind. Use weighty, substantial hinges on interior and entry doors, and save decorative butterfly hinges for cabinetry.
• Know the thickness of your door to determine the width of the hinge leaves. Note which side it is hinged on and whether it swings in or out. Some old hinges are not reversible.

What to avoid
• Incomplete sets. Make sure you have both hinge plates and the center pin, and that the hinge pivots smoothly. If the hinge sticks, graphite or lubricating oil may help.
• Mismatched finishes. You'll rarely find more than a half-dozen pieces in the same pattern and finish. If you're outfitting more than one room, consider using a different look for each.

Expect to pay About $20 per pair for steeple-tip cast-iron door hinges, and $50 or more for large brass ones cast with floral or geometric motifs.

A large Art Nouveau chandelier highlights this lofty ceiling.

Lighting ➤➤

Most of what you'll find are pendants and sconces made in the 1920s, '30s, and '40s, when companies mass-produced them for the millions of new homes being wired for electricity; previously, fixtures were fueled by gas and had open flames. The styles of these lights run the gamut from a hammered-copper porch lantern with an amber-color shade to a twinkling chandelier dripping with crystal teardrops. Restored fixtures that have been rewired and are ready to install can cost twice as much as unrestored ones.

How to shop
• Choose lights that match the architecture of the room. The clean lines of a flush-mount ceiling light with a single milky white shade fits with Art Deco–era and modern interiors. But it'd be out of place in Victorian-style spaces; those call for a fussier cast-brass chandelier with multiple outstretched arms.
• Coordinate the color of a glass shade with furniture, paint, or an area rug in the room to marry your lighting and decorating schemes.
• For exterior sconces and lanterns, look for fixture bodies made of weather-resistant metals, such as copper, bronze, and brass. These

require polishing but won't rust.

• Consider the use. A couple of pendant-style schoolhouse or industrial lights grouped above a kitchen island are great for task lighting. For an ambient glow in a bedroom, a flush-mount ceiling fixture or multi-arm chandelier is ideal. In the bathroom, sconces hung on either side of a mirrored medicine chest will cast fewer shadows on the face than an overhead light.

What to avoid

• Fixtures with missing parts. Reproduction shades, crystals, hanging chains, and ceiling or wall escutcheons that cover mounting hardware can be pricey, and you likely won't find an exact match to the original. For a five-light chandelier that's missing just one shade, for instance, you may have to buy all new replacements in a different style.

• An unrestored light with frayed wiring or a worn socket. These can be bargains, but you must rewire the fixture yourself or have a pro do it before you install it. You can find parts at lamp supply shops.

• An indoor fixture to use on a porch or front entry. In addition to being made from more durable metals than many indoor lights, outdoor ones should have a noncorrosive weatherproof socket covered by a protective metal housing.

Expect to pay $125 to $750 for a restored interior pendant with a glass shade. Crystal chandeliers start at $250 and go to $1,000 or more, depending on size and decoration. Restored sconces start about $250 per pair.

HOW TO SWAP IN A VINTAGE LIGHT

All you need to replace a ho-hum fixture with a stylish salvaged one are a ladder, screwdriver, wire nuts, and circuit tester. Here's how:

1. Cut power to the existing light at the breaker. Use a circuit tester to ensure that there's no electricity flowing.

2. Unscrew the nuts on the fixture's housing (a), and disconnect the hot black, neutral white, and bare ground wires in the electrical box from those on the light.

3. Install a new, universal mounting bracket (available at home centers) using the hardware provided. Heavy lights may require extra bracing in the ceiling.

4. Connect the white, black, and ground wires in the box to the vintage fixture's corresponding wires by twisting the ends together and screwing on wire nuts (b).

5. Secure the fixture to the mounting bracket, using the nuts provided. Screw in a bulb, and put on the shade (c).

6. Turn the power back on at the breaker, and flip the switch on your new old light.

Resources

➥ ARCHITECTURAL SALVAGE YARDS AND
REUSE CENTERS AROUND THE COUNTRY

Alabama
Southern Accents
Architectural Antiques
  Cullman, AL
  877-737-0554
  antiques-architectural.com

California
Architectural Salvage of
San Diego
  San Diego, CA
  619-696-1313
  architecturalsalvagesd.com
Gayle's Pasadena
Architectural Salvage
  Pasadena, CA
  626-535-9655
  *pasadenaarchitectural
  salvage.com*
Ohmega Salvage
  Berkeley, CA
  510-204-0767
  ohmegasalvage.com

Colorado
Architectural Artifacts
  Denver, CO
  303-296-0925
  architectural-artifacts.com
ReSource
  Boulder, CO
  303-419-5418
  resourceyard.org

Connecticut
United House Wrecking
  Stamford, CT
  203-348-5371
  unitedhousewrecking.com

District of Columbia
The Brass Knob
Architectural Antiques
  Washington, DC
  202-332-3370
  thebrassknob.com

Florida
Allison's Adam and Eve
Architectural Salvage
  West Palm Beach, FL
  561-655-1022
  adamandevesalvage.com
Florida Victorian
Architectural Antiques
  DeLand, FL
  386-734-9300
  floridavictorian.com
Sarasota
Architectural Salvage
  Sarasota, FL
  941-362-0803
  sarasotasalvage.com

Georgia
Pinch of the Past
Architectural Antiques
  Savannah, GA
  912-232-5563
  pinchofthepast.com
Re Use the Past
  Grantville, GA
  770-583-3111
  reusethepast.com

Illinois
Salvage One
  Chicago, IL
  312-733-0098
  salvageone.com
Urban Remains
  Chicago, IL
  312-492-6254
  urbanremainschicago.com

Indiana
Doc's Architectural
Salvage & Reclamation
Services
  Indianapolis, IN
  317-924-4000
  *docsarchitecturalsalvage
  .com*

Iowa
West End
Architectural Salvage
  Des Moines, IA
  515-243-0499
  westendarchsalvage.com

Kentucky
Cowgirl Attic
  Lexington, KY
  859-225-3876
  cowgirlattic.com

Louisiana
The Bank Architectural
Antiques
  New Orleans, LA
  504-523-2702
  thebankantiques.com
The Green Project
  New Orleans, LA
  504-945-0240
  thegreenproject.org

Maine
FIFI'S
  Augusta, ME
  207-623-0434
  fifisalvage.com
Old House Parts
Company
  Kennebunk, ME
  207-985-1999
  oldhouseparts.com
Portland Architectural
Salvage
  Portland, ME
  207-780-0634
  portlandsalvage.com

Maryland
Second Chance
  Baltimore, MD
  410-385-1101
  secondchanceinc.org

Massachusetts
New England
Demolition & Salvage
  New Bedford, MA
  508-992-1099
  nedsalvage.com

Michigan
Architectural Salvage
Warehouse of Detroit
  Detroit, MI
  248-254-2648
  aswdetroit.org
Materials Unlimited
  Ypsilanti, MI
  800-299-9462
  materialsunlimited.com
Sunset Junque Shop
  South Haven, MI
  269-637-5777
  sunsetjunque.com

Minnesota

Architectural Antiques
  Minneapolis, MN
  612-332-8344
  archantiques.com

Missouri

**Antiquities & Oddities
Architectural Salvage**
  Kansas City, MO
  816-283-3740
  *aoarchitecturalsalvage
  .com*
**Cross Creek
Architectural Artifacts**
  Springfield, MO
  417-890-7966
  crosscreekartifacts.com
**Foundation Architectural
Reclamation**
  Kansas City, MO
  816-283-8990
  foundationkc.com

Nebraska

A&R Salvage and Recycling
  Omaha, NB
  402-346-4470
  arsalvage.com

New Hampshire

Admac Salvage
  Littleton, NH
  603-444-1200
  admacsalvage.com
Architectural Salvage Inc.
  Exeter, NH
  603-773-5635
  oldhousesalvage.com

New Jersey

Recycling the Past
  Barnegat, NJ
  609-660-9790
  recyclingthepast.com

New York

Demolition Depot
  New York, NY
  212-860-1138
  demolitiondepot.com
**ReHouse
Architectural Salvage**
  Rochester, NY
  585-288-3080
  rehouseny.com
Significant Elements
  Ithaca, NY
  607-277-3450
  significantelements.org
Zaborski Emporium
  Kingston, NY
  845-338-6465
  stanthejunkman.com

North Carolina

**Architectural Salvage of
Greensboro**
  Greensboro, NC
  336-389-9118
  blandwood.org

Ohio

B&R Architectural Salvage
  Youngstown, OH
  330-747-2907
  brarchitecturalsalvage
  .com
Building Value
  Cincinnati, OH
  513-475-6783
  buildingvalue.org

Oregon

**Aurora Mills
Architectural Salvage**
  Aurora, OR
  503-678-6083
  auroramills.com
Bring
  Eugene, OR
  541-746-3023
  bringrecycling.org
**Hippo Hardware &
Trading Co.**
  Portland, OR
  503-231-1444
  hippohardware.com

Pennsylvania

Olde Good Things
  Scranton, PA
  888-233-9678
  ogtstore.com
Provenance
  Philadelphia, PA
  215-925-2002
  phillyprovenance.com

South Carolina

Architectural Warehouse
  Landrum, SC
  864-457-2199
  *architecturalwarehouse
  .com*
Old House Salvage
  Piedmont, SC
  864-787-2119
  theoldhousesalvage.com

Tennessee

Preservation Station
  Nashville, TN
  615-292-3595
  *thepreservationstation
  .com*

Texas

**Adkins Architectural
Antiques & Treasures**
  Houston, TX
  713-522-6547
  adkinsantiques.com
**Discovery Architectural
Antiques**
  Gonzales, TX
  830-672-2428
  discoverys.net

Utah

**George's
Architectural Salvage**
  Salt Lake City, UT
  801-539-1140
  georgessalvage.com

Vermont

**Architectural Salvage
Warehouse**
  Essex Junction, VT
  802-879-4221
  greatsalvage.com
**ReNew Building
Materials & Salvage**
  Brattleboro, VT
  802-246-2400
  renewsalvage.org

Virginia

**Architectural Old
House Parts**
  Front Royal, VA
  540-636-7984
  oldhouseparts.net
Black Dog Salvage
  Roanoke, VA
  540-343-6200
  blackdogsalvage.com
Caravati's Inc.
  Richmond, VA
  804-232-4175
  caravatis.com

Washington

**Earthwise
Architectural Salvage**
  Seattle, WA
  206-624-4510
  earthwise-salvage.com
Seattle Building Salvage
  Seattle, WA
  425-374-2550
  *seattlebuildingsalvage
  .com*
Second Use
  Seattle, WA
  206-763-6929
  seconduse.com

Wisconsin

Salvage Heaven
  Milwaukee, WI
  414-482-0286
  salvageheaven.com

ISBN-10: 0-8487-3540-4
ISBN-13: 978-0-8487-3540-1
Library of Congress Control Number: 2011929380

Printed in the United States of America
First Printing 2011

Oxmoor House

VP, Publishing Director: Jim Childs
Editorial Director: Susan Payne Dobbs
Brand Manager: Fonda Hitchcock
Managing Editor: Laurie S. Herr

TOH Salvage-Style Projects

Editor: Kathryn Keller
Art Director: Jennifer Procopio
Technical Editor: Mark Powers
Photo Editor: Allison Chin
Designer: Paris Osgerchian
Managing Editor: Jeff Nesmith
Editorial Production Manager: Yoshiko Taniguchi-Canada
Copy Editor: Alan Lockwood
Research Editor: Ambrose Martos
Proofreader: Timothy E. Pitt
Interns: Ben Macauley, Elsa Säätelä
Prepress Coordinator: Al Rufino
Design and Prepress Manager: Ann-Michelle Gallero
Book Production Manager: Susan Chodakiewicz

Our thanks to Amy Rosenfeld and Edward Potokar for their
help creating, styling, and photographing many of the salvage
projects shown in this book.

To order additional publications, call 1-800-765-6400
or 1-800-491-0551.

For more books to enrich your life, visit oxmoorhouse.com.

To subscribe to *This Old House* magazine, go to
thisoldhouse.com/customerservice or call 1-800-898-7237.

This Old House Magazine

Editor: Scott Omelianuk
Publisher: Charles R. Kammerer

EDITORIAL

Deputy Editor: Kathryn Keller
Managing Editor: Jeff Nesmith
Building Technology Editor: Thomas Baker
Design Editor: Colette Scanlon
Features Editor: Amy R. Hughes
Articles Editor: Deborah Baldwin
Senior Editor: Deborah Snoonian
Senior Technical Editor: Mark Powers
Staff Editor: Jessica Dodell-Feder
Associate Editor: Keith Pandolfi
Assistant Editors: Sal Vaglica, Jennifer Stimpson, Danielle Blundell
Copy Chief: Timothy E. Pitt
Deputy Copy Chief: Leslie Monthan
Special Projects Editor: Eric Hagerman
Senior Contributor: Mark Feirer
Editorial Assistant and Assistant to the Editor: Gillian Barth

ART

Design Director: Hylah Hill
Art Director: Jennifer Procopio
Director of Photography: Denise Sfraga
Deputy Art Director: Douglas Adams
Associate Photo Editor: Allison Chin
Designer: Paris Osgerchian
Art/Online Assistant: Robert Hardin
Editorial Production Manager: Yoshiko Taniguchi-Canada

ONLINE

Online Editor: Alexandra Bandon
Web Designer: Bill Mazza
Associate Editor: Tabitha Sukhai
Contributing Producer: Amanda Keiser

EDITORIAL BOARD

Master Carpenter: Norm Abram
General Contractor: Tom Silva
Plumbing and Heating Expert: Richard Trethwey
Landscape Contractor: Roger Cook
Host: Kevin O'Connor

Photography Credits

Cover: (bottom left) Matthew Benson **Back cover:** (right) Joshua Paul **p. 3:** Ryan Benyi **p. 4:** (top right) Amy Rosenfeld **p. 5:** (top) Ryan Benyi
p. 6: (top to bottom) Wyatt McSpadden; Ryan Benyi **p. 7:** (top and middle) Ryan Benyi **p. 8:** (bottom) Sarah Wilson **p. 9:** (left) Keller & Keller; (top right) Sarah
Wilson **p. 10:** Ryan Benyi **p. 11:** Beth Perkins **p. 12:** Ryan Benyi **p. 13:** Russell Kaye **pp. 14–15:** (clockwise from top left) Don Penny/Time Inc. Digital Studio;
Ted Morrison (4); Don Penny/Time Inc. Digital Studio; Ted Morrison **p. 17:** Matthew Benson **p. 19:** (bottom) Ted Morrison **p. 27:** (right) Julian Wass
p. 30: (bottom) Erik Johnson **p. 46:** (bottom) Kenneth Chen **p. 48:** Deborah Whitlaw Llewellyn **pp. 57–59:** Amy Rosenfeld **p. 58:** (bottom) Joshua Paul
p. 71: (right) Sarah Wilson **p. 75:** (right) Sarah Wilson **pp. 76–77:** Alise O'Brien **p. 83:** (right) Kenneth Chen **p. 86:** (bottom) Joshua Paul **p. 97:** (right) Joshua Paul
pp. 104–105: Nathan Kirkman **p. 111:** (right) Sarah Wilson **p. 119:** (right) Joshua Paul **p. 125:** (right) Allison Dinner **p. 135:** (clockwise from top left) Ken Gutmaker;
Julian Wass; Deborah Whitlaw Llewellyn **p. 136:** Keith Scott Morton **p. 137:** (left to right) J. Savage Gibson; Don Penny/Time Inc. Digital Studio
p. 138: Timothy Bell **p. 139:** (left to right) Wyatt McSpadden; Paul Whicheloe **p. 140:** Timothy Bell **p. 141:** Cressida Payavis